Senior Editor: Julia Moore
Associate Editor: Victoria Craven-Cohn
Designer: David Brier
Letterers: Edward E. Benguiat & David Brier
Page Makeup: Jay Anning
Photographer: Dennis Williford
Production Manager: Ellen Greene
Compositor: Trufont Typographers, Inc.
Set in Brittanic and ITC New Baskerville Italic

CONTENTS

Edward E. Benguiat
Chairperson, TDC 33

CHAIRPERSON'S STATEMENT

EDWARD E. BENGUIAT

*Vice President, Creative Director
Photo-Lettering, Inc.
New York, New York*

Since the first TDC annual in 1953, the profession of graphic design in typography has exploded into a highly competitive industry. Over the years, the Type Directors Club has consistently set forth one primary goal: to preserve and foster excellence in typographic design for one and all.

The jury of the 33rd annual competition of the Type Directors Club was responsible for evaluating over 4,000 entries from around the world. The judges themselves were all multiple-award-winning design and typography professionals with high-caliber standards that made the selection of the pieces very difficult.

✿

Ed Benguiat earned his B.A. in music at Brooklyn College and worked as a successful jazz drummer for many years before becoming interested in a career in the graphic arts. After studying at Columbia University and the Workshop of Advertising Art in New York City, Benguiat was soon designing letterforms and logotypes and has worked as a designer and art director at many of the major advertising agencies and publishing houses in New York City.

Benguiat, who has won many awards for his typography, is well known for his many typeface designs. More than ninety-two alphabets in the ITC collection are the result of his creative talents.

Presently Vice President, Creative Director at Photo-Lettering, Inc., where he has been employed since 1962, Benguiat also teaches at The School of Visual Arts, continues to create and design letterforms, and flies his own racing plane.

He is a member of the Type Directors Club, the New York Art Directors Club, and the Alliance Graphic Internationale.

1 Norbert Florendo
2 Jane Opiat
3 Bonnie Hazelton
4 Louise Fili
5 Richard Wilde
6 Tony DiSpigna
7 Ernie Smith

THE JUDGES

TONY DI SPIGNA

*Graphic Designer and
Letterform Illustrator
Tony DiSpigna, Inc.
New York, New York*

*Too often in visual communication
typography becomes a mechanical
addendum instead of a creative
expression that contributes to the
effectiveness of the design. Thus it
was gratifying to see that some
designers and art directors are
taking type seriously and using it
as an integral design element.*

*While judging entries at
TDC 33, I quickly passed over
pieces that were simply clichés. I
also passed over the slick, elaborate
production pieces that could have
been entrants to a "Guess Who
Spent the Most Money" contest.
These pieces had flash and glitter
but no substance or structure. In
cases where the letterform and
typographic treatment are the dom-
inant visual element, the problem
of judging became one of being
able to discern between excellent
solutions and poor imitations. I
chose those solutions that were both
well conceived and professionally
executed. A successful product
is inevitable when good design is
combined with excellent typography.*

Tony DiSpigna, *a graduate of
New York City Community College
and Pratt Institute, joined
Lubalin, Smith & Carnase, Inc.*

*in 1969 as a typographic and
letterform designer. It was here he
gained valuable experience in all
areas of visual communication.*

*In 1973 he opened his own
studio in New York City. His
designs have appeared in various
trade publications and have won
many awards from such prestigious organizations as the Art
Directors Club, The One Show,
American Institute of Graphic
Arts, and The Creativity Shows.*

*DiSpigna has designed nu-
merous typefaces, most notably
Serif Gothic, Playgirl, Fattoni,
Lubalin Graph, and an exclusive
typeface for Channel 13 WNET
public television station in New
York City.*

*In 1978, DiSpigna joined
Herb Lubalin Associates as a vice
president and partner, and, in
1980, became independent and
opened his own design firm, Tony
DiSpigna, Inc. In addition to
running his design firm, DiSpigna
is also currently an assistant
professor at Pratt Institute teach
ing typography and typographics
in its graduate program, and a
teacher at The School of Visual Arts
and at The New York Institute
of Technology.*

LOUISE FILI

*Art Director
Pantheon Books
New York, New York*
Four thousand entries later, the

*notion of good typography is an
enigma. The judging process
makes it necessary to isolate typography from its context—printing,
paper stock, illustration, photography—aspects that can easily seduce
a juror. One hopes that the selection shown here reflects the most
inclusive criteria.*

Louise Fili *has been art director
of Pantheon Books since 1978.
She has won numerous awards for
book cover design, including a
gold and silver medal from The
Art Directors Club. She teaches a
senior portfolio course at The
School of Visual Arts and at The
Cooper Union.*

NORBERT FLORENDO

*Creative Director,
Graphic Products Group
Compugraphic Corporation
Wilmington, Massachusetts*
*What I felt most encouraged about
while viewing the TDC 33 entries
was an emerging passion for the
dynamic power of type. This was
evident in the wide variety of
approaches used to meet the chal-
lenge of placing type meaningfully
on paper.*

*Typography is also looking
back, as it often does, for creative
inspiration from the past. It's as if
our young designers are decipher-
ing the typographic logic behind
the intimately handcrafted composition of the letterpress era and*

are molding it with the precision and versatility of the electronic digital and laser typesetting systems of today. I was proud to participate as a juror, and I believe my greatest reward was the opportunity to experience the wealth of typographic designs submitted from around the world.

❧

Norbert Florendo, a graduate of The Cooper Union, is responsible for the selection and development of all new and licensed typeface designs produced for Compugraphic Corporation both domestically and internationally. His tasks include directing their type design team as well as working with type foundries, designers, and typographers worldwide.

As Compugraphics' former art director and advertising manager, his works have received honors from the Type Directors Club, DESI awards, National Composition Association, and Art Directors Club of Boston. He is also an active member of the TDC and has served as its Traveling Show Chairperson.

many years, I was honored to be chosen as a judge for TDC 33.

I was impressed that classic and calligraphic styles appear to be in vogue once again. Even the annual report formats seem to be departing from the expected formulas in exciting ways.

My only disappointment was that some of the pieces had all the right ingredients, as far as design was concerned, but lacked basic good typography.

❧

Bonnie Hazelton is Vice President, Director of Typography at McCann-Erickson, New York. She has been an active member of the TDC for over ten years, and has served on the board in various offices, including President and Chairperson.

Hazelton graduated from SUATC, Farmingdale, New York, with an Associate's degree in advertising art and design, and worked in typography at various ad agencies before joining McCann-Erickson in 1979.

She has won several TDC awards for her typography and has co-chaired the TDC Annual Competition.

Thanks for the vote of confidence. It was truly an honor to have the opportunity to be with other typography fanatics and to have my knowledge and love of type tested and confirmed. Being a judge provided me with the opportunity to express my commitment toward excellence of typography.

It was hard work, physically and mentally. Imagine scrutinizing over 4,000 entries over a two-day period and giving each piece the undivided and individual attention it deserved. The manner in which the judging was handled was well organized and the procedures went smoothly. My thanks to all the volunteers and to the Type Directors Club. It was truly a pleasant and memorable experience.

❧

Jane Opiat graduated from the University of Santa Barbara with a B.A. in painting and art history. She has been with Lord, Geller, Federico, Einstein, Inc. since 1982.

ERNIE SMITH

BONNIE HAZELTON

*Vice President
Director of Typography
McCann-Erickson, Inc.
New York, New York*
As an active participant in the Type Directors Club and its previous annual competitions for

JANE OPIAT

*Type Director
Lord, Geller, Federico, Einstein, Inc.
New York, New York*
I was extremely flattered to be asked to be a judge for TDC 33.

*Executive Vice President/
Creative Director of Art
Sudler & Hennessey
New York, New York*
The invitation to judge TDC 33 was not only an honor and an opportunity to get a first-hand look at what is going on with typographic design but a welcome chance to see some wonderful friends and colleagues from days

gone by. It was amazing how my friends and colleagues seem not to age while my own mirror tells me I am living the September years.

The work we judged was of the highest quality, and it was a real joy to look at so many good pieces. Some of the work was truly striking and brilliant. The range of design styles ran the gamut, although new wave and lots of letterspacing dominated.

I related particularly well to the TDC's system of judging. It was very fair and thoughtful. Every piece was considered separately, with each juror making an individual and anonymous decision. The committee was incredibly efficient and organized. It was a pleasure to play a part in assembling this typographic time capsule.

❧

Ernie Smith is currently Creative Director, Executive Vice President of Creative Medical Communications, a division of Sudler & Hennessey where he has worked since 1978.

After graduating from the Art Center School, Los Angeles, in 1952, Smith started his career with Sudler & Hennessey, left to join Herb Lubalin, Inc. as Partner, Vice President, and then rejoined Sudler & Hennessey as Associate Creative Director, Executive Vice President.

Smith has won numerous awards from AIGA, Type Directors Club, and Communications Arts and has been published in Graphis magazine.

In addition to his successful career as a graphic designer, Smith is a renowned jazz/jazz dance historian, film collector, archivist, consultant, lecturer, and an accomplished painter.

RICHARD WILDE

Head of Advertising
Graphic Design
Co-chairperson of the Media
Arts Department
The School of Visual Arts
New York, New York

The notion of typographic excellence is an intriguing one. Judging approximately 4,000 entries can be an overwhelming task. One must learn to judge as a wine taster, remembering to cleanse the palate after each sampling. The idea of beauty and formal concerns seemed to be the overriding issues. Concept, for the most part, took a supporting role.

On judging, I simply tried to let each piece impress itself upon me. The initial impression, if any, was usually emotional in quality and was the crucial factor in identifying typographic excellence. This was quickly followed by a mental interpretation. Yet it was this very first impression that truly signaled its significance.

I soon began to see which typographic solutions had a life beyond their intended messages and which pieces didn't. It was evident to me that the quiet typographic revolution lives on.

❧

Richard Wilde has served for the past sixteen years as Co-chairperson of the Media Arts department, Head of Graphic Design and Ad-

vertising at The School of Arts, and has also worked director for the Visual Art.

He has taught graph sign, advertising, and exp tal design workshops at Pr Institute, the University of at Austin, the National Co Art and Design in Ireland the Communication School Hong Kong.

Wilde is a contributing editor to How Magazine *and the author of* Problems/Solutions: Visual Thinking for Graphic Communicators. *He has won many awards in both advertising and design and his work has appeared in many of the major annuals.*

He is a member of the AIGA and of the Art Directors Club of New York for which he is currently Treasurer and also serves on the Executive Committee.

TYPOGRAPHY 8

THE EIGHTH ANNUAL OF THE TYPE DIRECTORS CLUB

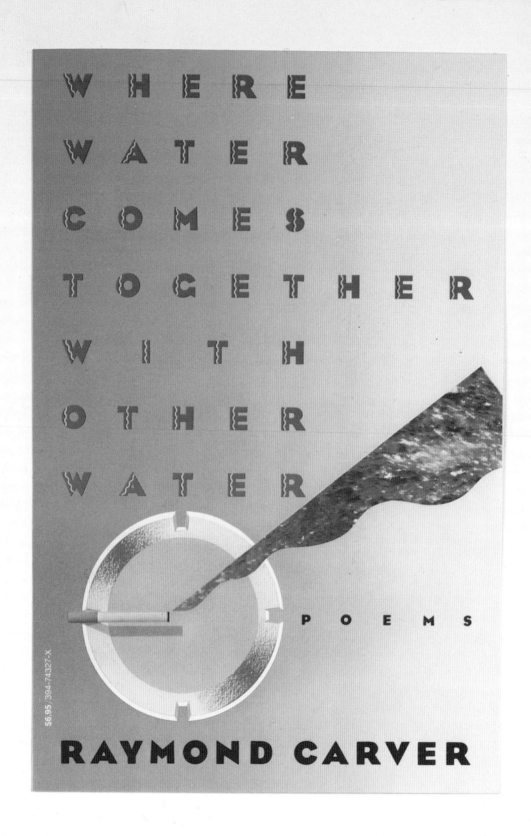

BOOK COVER
TYPOGRAPHY/DESIGN *Carin Goldberg, New York, New York* **TYPOGRAPHIC SUPPLIER** *The Type Shop* **STUDIO** *Carin Goldberg Design*
CLIENT *Vintage Books* **PRINCIPAL TYPE** *Eagle Bold* **DIMENSIONS** *5³/₁₆ × 8 in. (13.2 × 20.3 cm).*

THIS BOOK ANNOUNCES OUR 1987 FIRST BANK SYSTEM MANAGEMENT CONFERENCE · THE WORDS AND IMAGES YOU FIND HERE REIN-FORCE THE WORK WE WILL BEGIN TOGETHER ON MONDAY MORNING, FEBRUARY 9TH · WE INVITE YOU AND YOUR SPOUSE OR GUEST TO JOIN US FOR PARTNERS IN PERFORMANCE AT MARRIOTT CITY CEN-TER, MINNEAPOLIS

PARTNERS IN PERFORMANCE FIRST BANK SYSTEM 1987

BOOK
TYPOGRAPHY/DESIGN *Charles Spencer Anderson, Minneapolis, Minnesota* **TYPOGRAPHIC SUPPLIER** *Great Faces*
STUDIO *Duffy Design Group* **CLIENT** *First Bank System* **PRINCIPAL TYPE** *Eagle Bold* **DIMENSIONS** *4⅝ × 7¼in. (11.7 × 18.4 cm).*

RECORD ALBUM COVER
TYPOGRAPHY/DESIGN *Carin Goldberg, New York, New York* **STUDIO** *Carin Goldberg Design* **CLIENT** *Nonesuch Records*
PRINCIPAL TYPE *Meese Grotesk Solid* **DIMENSIONS** *12³/₈ × 12³/₈ in. (31.4 × 31.4 cm).*

BOOK JACKET
TYPOGRAPHY/DESIGN *Carin Goldberg, New York, New York* **TYPOGRAPHIC SUPPLIER** *The Type Shop* **STUDIO** *Carin Goldberg Design*
CLIENT *Alfred A. Knopf* **PRINCIPAL TYPES** *Washington and Eagle Bold* **DIMENSIONS** *6⁵/₁₆ × 9⁷/₁₆ in. (16 × 24 cm).*

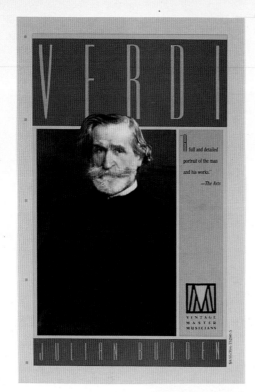

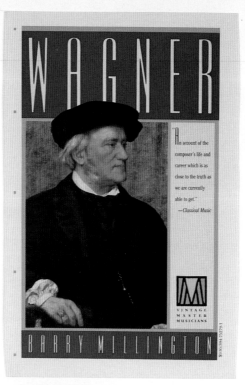

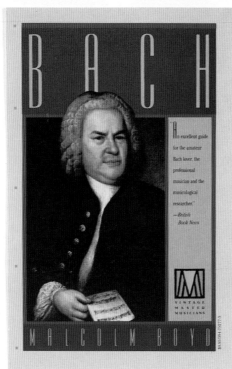

BOOK COVERS
TYPOGRAPHY/DESIGN *Carin Goldberg, New York, New York* **TYPOGRAPHIC SUPPLIER** *The Type Shop* **STUDIO** *Carin Goldberg Design*
CLIENT *Vintage Books* **PRINCIPAL TYPE** *Empire* **DIMENSIONS** *5³/₁₆ × 8 in. (14 × 21.6 cm).*

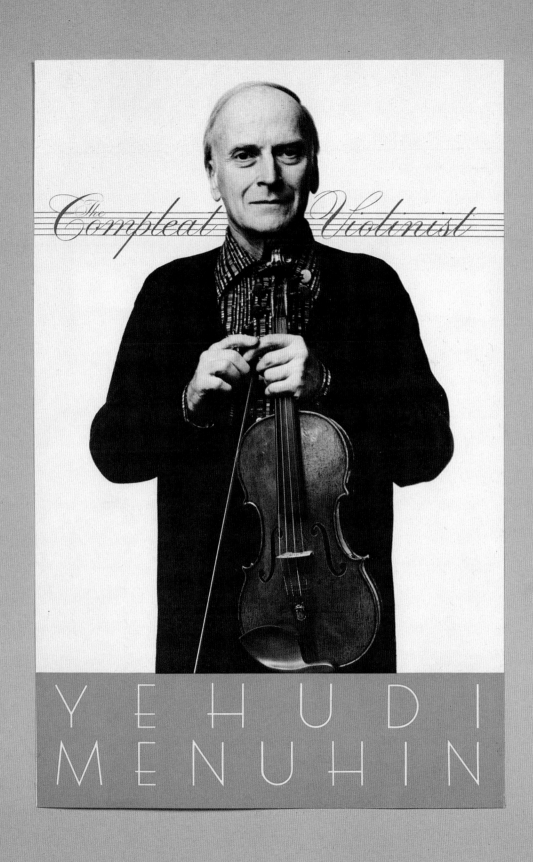

BOOK JACKET
TYPOGRAPHY/DESIGN *Louise Fili, New York, New York* **LETTERER** *Louise Fili* **TYPOGRAPHIC SUPPLIER** *Photo-Lettering, Inc.*
CLIENT *Simon & Schuster* **PRINCIPAL TYPES** *Rigoletto Script and handlettering* **DIMENSIONS** *5½ × 8½ in. (14 × 21.6 cm).*

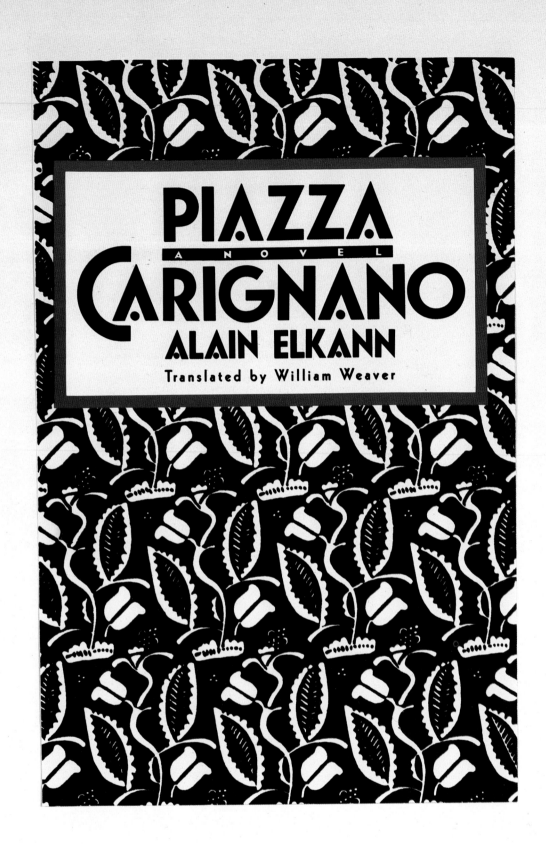

BOOK JACKET

TYPOGRAPHY/DESIGN *Louise Fili, New York, New York* **LETTERER** *Louise Fili* **CLIENT** *Atlantic Monthly Press* **PRINCIPAL TYPE** *Handlettering* **DIMENSIONS** *5¹/₂ × 8¹/₂ in. (14 × 21.6 cm).*

LOGOTYPE
TYPOGRAPHY/DESIGN *James Wageman, New York, New York* **LETTERER** *Tom Carnase, New York, New York* **CLIENT** *Abbeville Press*
PRINCIPAL TYPE *Jocunda (modified).*

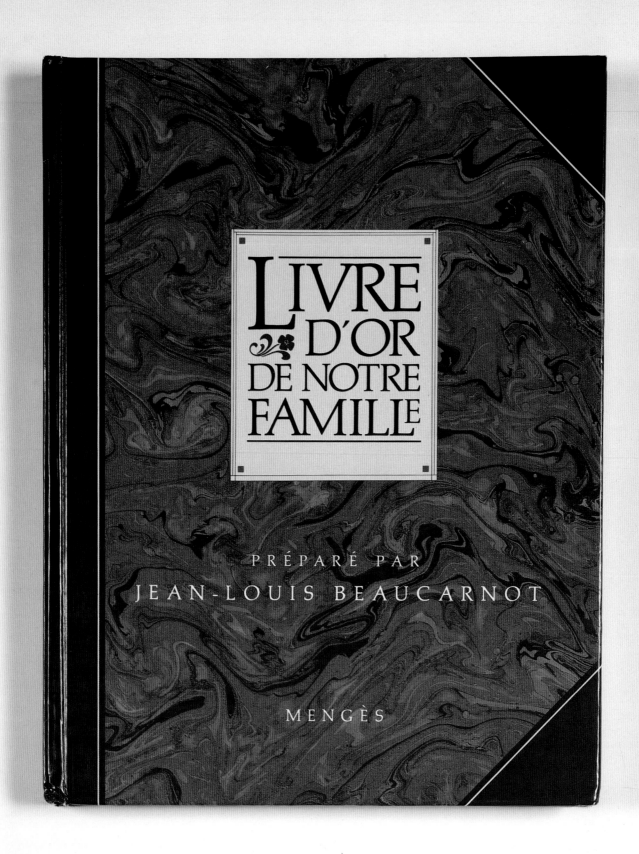

BOOK
TYPOGRAPHY/DESIGN *Ernesto Aparicio, Paris, France* **TYPOGRAPHIC SUPPLIER** *SCG* **STUDIO** *Ernesto Aparicio Design*
CLIENT *Editions Mengès* **PRINCIPAL TYPE** *Palatino* **DIMENSIONS** *8½ × 10⅞ in. (21.5 × 27.6 cm).*

State of the School

1986

𝖂harton
The Wharton School • University of Pennsylvania

BROCHURE
TYPOGRAPHY/DESIGN *Robert J. Warkulwiz, Michael Rogalski, and William F. Smith Jr., Philadelphia, Pennsylvania*
LETTERER *Rosie Stars, Gloucester City, New Jersey* **TYPOGRAPHIC SUPPLIER** *PHP Typography* **STUDIO** *Warkulwiz Design Associates*
CLIENT *The Wharton School* **PRINCIPAL TYPE** *Caslon 540* **DIMENSIONS** *8½ × 11 in. (21.6 × 27.9 cm).*

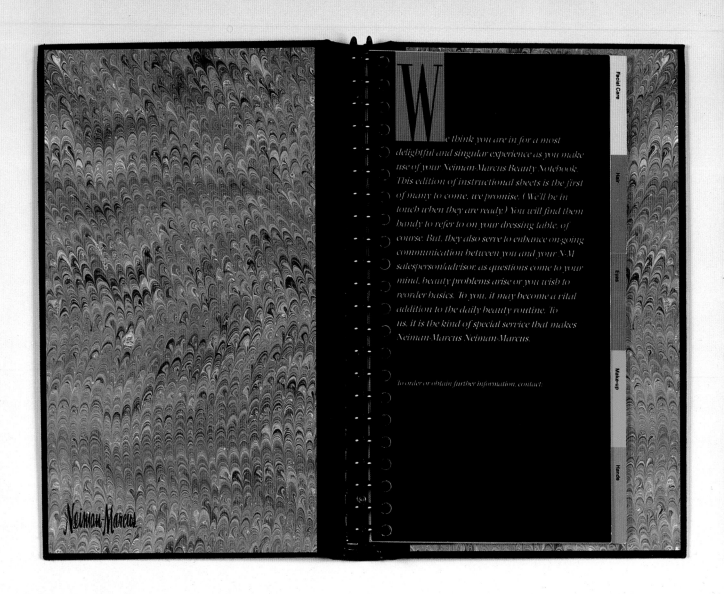

BOOK
TYPOGRAPHY/DESIGN *Don Sibley and Steve Gibbs, Dallas, Texas* **TYPOGRAPHIC SUPPLIER** *Robert J. Hilton Co., Inc.*
STUDIO *Sibley/Peteet Design, Inc.* **CLIENT** *Neiman-Marcus* **PRINCIPAL TYPES** *Garamond Book and Helvetica Medium*
DIMENSIONS *7¼ × 11⅝ in. (18.4 × 29.5 cm).*

BROCHURE
TYPOGRAPHY/DESIGN *Gary W. Priester, Novato, California* **TYPOGRAPHIC SUPPLIER** *Omnicomp* **AGENCY** *The Black Point Group*
CLIENT *Singer Printing, Inc.* **PRINCIPAL TYPES** *Various* **DIMENSIONS** *9 × 9 in. (22.9 × 22.9 cm).*

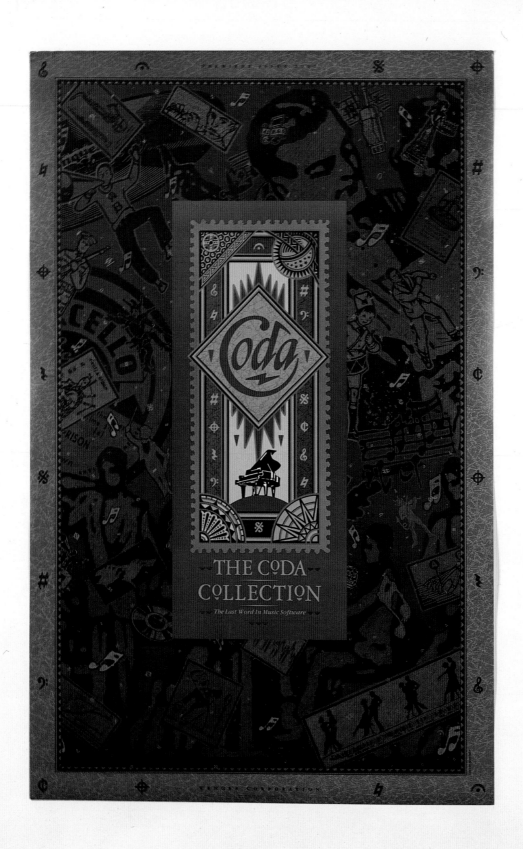

POSTER

TYPOGRAPHY/DESIGN *Charles Spencer Anderson, Minneapolis, Minnesota* **CALLIGRAPHERS** *Charles Spencer Anderson,*
Sara Ledgard, and Mitch Lindgren **TYPOGRAPHIC SUPPLIER** *Typeshooters* **STUDIO** *Duffy Design Group* **CLIENT** *Wenger Corporation*
PRINCIPAL TYPE *Goudy* **DIMENSIONS** *23 × 36 in. (58.4 × 91.4 cm).*

CATALOG

TYPOGRAPHY/DESIGN *Charles Spencer Anderson and Joe Duffy, Minneapolis, Minnesota* **CALLIGRAPHERS** *Charles Spencer Anderson and Mitch Lindgren* **TYPOGRAPHIC SUPPLIER** *Typeshooters* **STUDIO** *Duffy Design Group* **CLIENT** *Wenger Corporation* **PRINCIPAL TYPE** *Garamond* **DIMENSIONS** *11 × 7½ in. (27.9 × 19.1 cm).*

POSTER
TYPOGRAPHY/DESIGN *Charles Spencer Anderson, Minneapolis, Minnesota* **TYPOGRAPHIC SUPPLIER** *Typeshooters*
STUDIO *Duffy Design Group* **CLIENT** *Washburn Child Guidance Center* **PRINCIPAL TYPE** *Spire* **DIMENSIONS** *36 × 17 in.*
(91.2 × 43.2 cm).

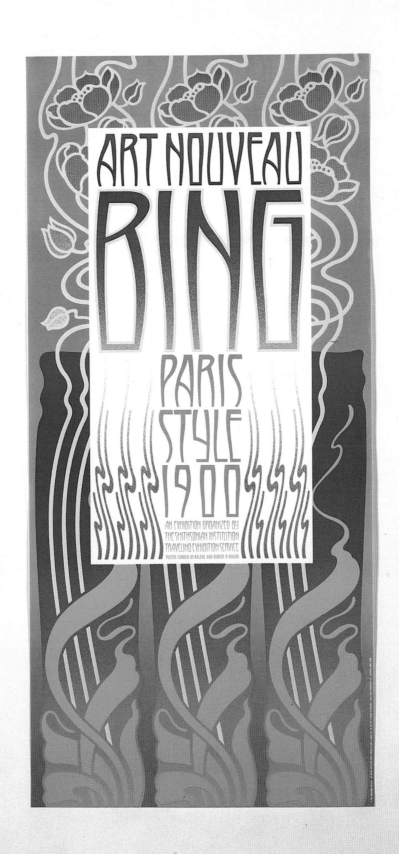

POSTER
TYPOGRAPHY/DESIGN *Daniel Pelavin, New York, New York* **LETTERER** *Daniel Pelavin* **STUDIO** *Grafik Communications Ltd.*
CLIENT *Smithsonian Institution* **PRINCIPAL TYPE** *Handlettering* **DIMENSIONS** *17 × 36 in. (43.2 × 91.5 cm).*

BROCHURE
TYPOGRAPHY/DESIGN *The Pushpin Group* **ART DIRECTOR** *Seymour Chwast, New York, New York* **TYPOGRAPHIC SUPPLIER** *Cardinal Type Service, Inc.* **STUDIO** *The Pushpin Group, Inc.* **CLIENT** *Mohawk Paper Mills, Inc.* **PRINCIPAL TYPES** *ITC Benguiat Gothic Book and Medium* **DIMENSIONS** *10⅛ × 12 in. (25.7 × 30.5 cm).*

CORPORATE IDENTITY
TYPOGRAPHY/DESIGN *Tim Girvin, Seattle, Washington* **LETTERERS** *Tim Girvin and Anton Kimball* **STUDIO** *Tim Girvin Design*
CLIENT *Peter Miller Books* **PRINCIPAL TYPE** *Handlettering.*

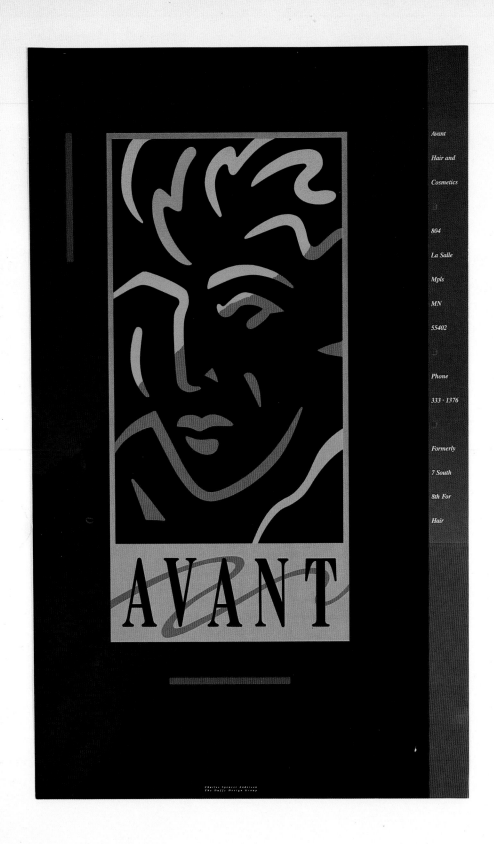

ANNOUNCEMENT
TYPOGRAPHY/DESIGN *Charles Spencer Anderson, Minneapolis, Minnesota* **LETTERER** *Lynne Schulte, Minneapolis, Minnesota*
TYPOGRAPHIC SUPPLIER *Typeshooters* **STUDIO** *Duffy Design Group* **CLIENT** *Avant Hair Salon* **PRINCIPAL TYPE** *Times Roman Condensed Customized* **DIMENSIONS** *31 × 18¾ in. (78.7 × 47.6 cm).*

ANNOUNCEMENT
TYPOGRAPHY/DESIGN *Charles Spencer Anderson, Minneapolis, Minnesota* **TYPOGRAPHIC SUPPLIER** *Typeshooters*
STUDIO *Duffy Design Group* **CLIENT** *Duffy Design Group* **PRINCIPAL TYPE** *Helvetica Bold* **DIMENSIONS** *8½ × 11 in. (21.6 × 27.9 cm).*

POSTER
TYPOGRAPHY/DESIGN *Charles Spencer Anderson, Minneapolis, Minnesota* **TYPOGRAPHIC SUPPLIER** *Typeshooters*
STUDIO *Duffy Design Group* **CLIENT** *Fresh Force Youth Volunteer Group* **PRINCIPAL TYPE** *Futura Condensed* **DIMENSIONS**
36 × 19⁷⁄₈ in. (91.4 × 50.2 cm).

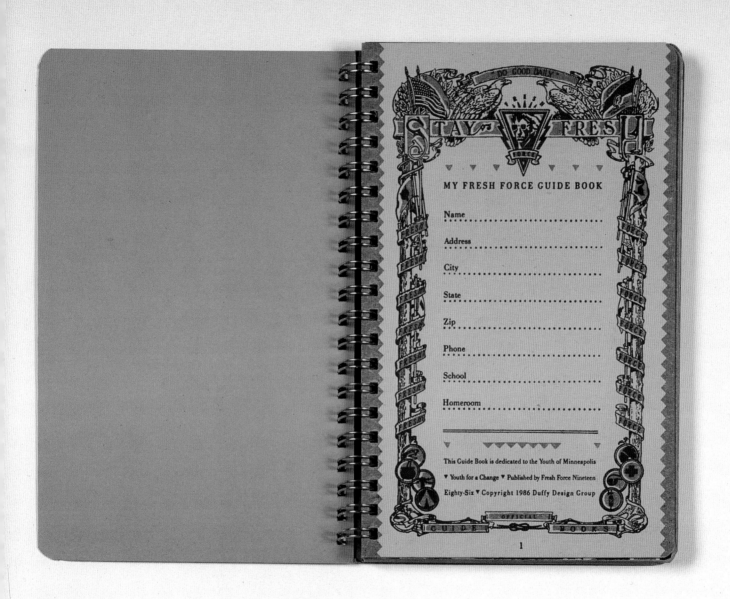

BOOK
TYPOGRAPHY/DESIGN *Charles Spencer Anderson, Minneapolis, Minnesota* **TYPOGRAPHIC SUPPLIER** *Typeshooters*
STUDIO *Duffy Design Group* **CLIENT** *Fresh Force Youth Volunteer Group* **PRINCIPAL TYPE** *Futura Condensed* **DIMENSIONS** *5 × 7 in.*
(12.7 × 17.8 cm).

POSTER
TYPOGRAPHY/DESIGN *Joe Duffy, Minneapolis, Minnesota* **TYPOGRAPHIC SUPPLIER** *Typeshooters* **STUDIO** *Duffy Design Group*
CLIENT *First Tennessee Bank* **PRINCIPAL TYPE** *Goudy* **DIMENSIONS** *38 × 20 in. (96.5 × 50.8 cm).*

POSTER
TYPOGRAPHY/DESIGN *Joe Duffy, Minneapolis, Minnesota* **TYPOGRAPHIC SUPPLIER** *Typeshooters* **STUDIO** *Duffy Design Group*
CLIENT *First Tennessee Bank* **PRINCIPAL TYPE** *Goudy Old Style Condensed* **DIMENSIONS** *38 × 20 in. (96.5 × 50.8 cm).*

This book from the French Paper Company displays two products: work from The Duffy Design Group of Minneapolis, and Speckletone paper. While our Speckletone swatch book shows you what's available, this book gives you ideas on what's possible. ■ Unlike paper with less textural character, Speckletone Cover and Text work with a design to create a feeling as well as an image. In printed areas, inks combine with Speckletone to build color into the paper, not just upon it. And in unprinted areas, Speckletone can transform negative space into a positive visual element. So it becomes more than a paper; it becomes a part of the design. ■ That's why we make Speckletone. Not to be just a surface where you tackle a design problem, but a design element to help you solve it.

BOOK
TYPOGRAPHY/DESIGN *Charles Spencer Anderson and Joe Duffy, Minneapolis, Minnesota* **TYPOGRAPHIC SUPPLIER** *Typeshooters*
STUDIO *Duffy Design Group* **CLIENT** *French Paper Company* **PRINCIPAL TYPE** *Garamond* **DIMENSIONS** *9 × 5⅞ in. (22.9 × 14.6 cm).*

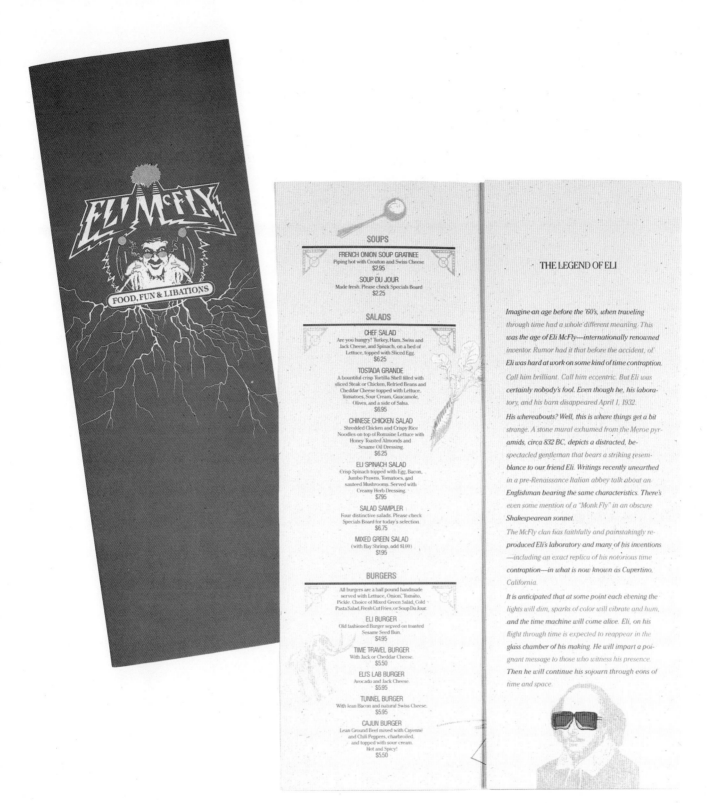

SOUPS

FRENCH ONION SOUP GRATINEE
Piping hot with Crouton and Swiss Cheese
$2.95

SOUP DU JOUR
Made fresh. Please check Specials Board
$2.25

SALADS

CHEF SALAD
Are you hungry? Turkey, Ham, Swiss and
Jack Cheese, and Spinach, on a bed of
Lettuce, topped with Sliced Egg.
$6.25

TOSTADA GRANDE
A bountiful crisp Tortilla Shell filled with
sliced Steak or Chicken, Refried Beans and
Cheddar Cheese topped with Lettuce,
Tomatoes, Sour Cream, Guacamole,
Olives, and a side of Salsa.
$6.95

CHINESE CHICKEN SALAD
Shredded Chicken and Crispy Rice
Noodles on top of Romaine Lettuce with
Honey Toasted Almonds and
Sesame Oil Dressing.
$6.25

ELI' SPINACH SALAD
Crisp Spinach topped with Egg, Bacon,
Jumbo Prawns, Tomatoes, and
sauteed Mushrooms. Served with
Creamy Herb Dressing.
$7.95

SALAD SAMPLER
Four distinctive salads. Please check
Specials Board for today's selection.
$6.75

MIXED GREEN SALAD
(with Bay Shrimp, add $1.00)
$1.95

BURGERS

All burgers are a half pound handmade
served with Lettuce, Onion, Tomato,
Pickle. Choice of Mixed Green Salad, Cold
Pasta Salad, Fresh Cut Fries, or Soup Du Jour.

ELI BURGER
Old fashioned Burger served on toasted
Sesame Seed Bun.
$4.95

TIME TRAVEL BURGER
With Jack or Cheddar Cheese.
$5.50

ELI'S LAB BURGER
Avocado and Jack Cheese.
$5.95

TUNNEL BURGER
With lean Bacon and natural Swiss Cheese.
$5.95

CAJUN BURGER
Lean Ground Beef mixed with Cayenne
and Chili Peppers, charbroiled,
and topped with sour cream.
Hot and Spicy!
$5.50

THE LEGEND OF ELI

Imagine an age before the '60's, when traveling through time had a whole different meaning. This was the age of Eli McFly—internationally renowned inventor. Rumor had it that before the accident, ol' Eli was hard at work on some kind of time contraption. Call him brilliant. Call him eccentric. But Eli was certainly nobody's fool. Even though he, his laboratory, and his barn disappeared April 1, 1932.

His whereabouts? Well, this is where things get a bit strange. A stone mural exhumed from the Meroe pyramids, circa 832 BC, depicts a distracted, bespectacled gentleman that bears a striking resemblance to our friend Eli. Writings recently unearthed in a pre-Renaissance Italian abbey talk about an Englishman bearing the same characteristics. There's even some mention of a "Monk Fly" in an obscure Shakespearean sonnet.

The McFly clan has faithfully and painstakingly reproduced Eli's laboratory and many of his inventions —including an exact replica of his notorious time contraption—in what is now known as Cupertino, California.

It is anticipated that at some point each evening the lights will dim, sparks of color will vibrate and hum, and the time machine will come alive. Eli, on his flight through time is expected to reappear in the glass chamber of his making. He will impart a poignant message to those who witness his presence. Then he will continue his sojourn through eons of time and space.

MENU
TYPOGRAPHY/DESIGN *Rick Tharp and Karen Nomura, Los Gatos, California* **ILLUSTRATORS** *Rick Tharp, Karen Nomura, and Mike Leeds*
TYPOGRAPHIC SUPPLIER *Metro Typography* **STUDIO** *THARP DID IT* **CLIENT** *Eli McFly* **PRINCIPAL TYPES** *Cheltenham and Helvetica*
DIMENSIONS *22 × 16 in. (56 × 40.6 cm).*

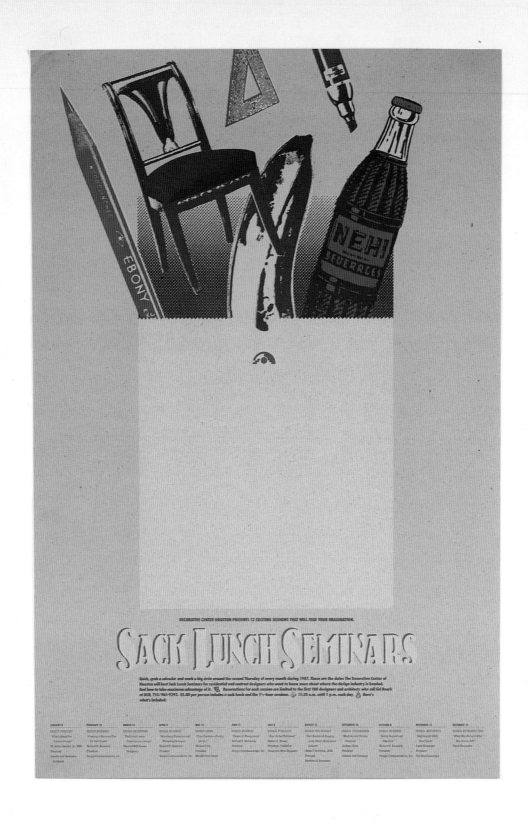

POSTER
TYPOGRAPHY/DESIGN *Mark Geer and Richard Kilmer, Houston, Texas* **TYPOGRAPHIC SUPPLIER** *Characters, Inc.* **AGENCY** *Boswell Byers*
STUDIO *Kilmer/Geer Design, Inc.* **CLIENT** *Decorative Center Houston* **PRINCIPAL TYPES** *Futura Extra Bold Condensed and ITC*
Cheltenham Book **DIMENSIONS** *20 × 30 in. (51 × 76.2 cm).*

POSTER
TYPOGRAPHY/DESIGN *James A. Houff and Nancy Kling, Detroit, Michigan* **ART DIRECTOR** *James A. Houff*
TYPOGRAPHIC SUPPLIER *Dick Martini Associates* **STUDIO** *WDIV/TV 4 Design Department* **CLIENT** *WDIV/TV 4*
PRINCIPAL TYPES *Various* **DIMENSIONS** *16 × 21½ (40.6 × 54.6 cm).*

ANNUAL REPORT

TYPOGRAPHY/DESIGN *John Hornall and Luann Bice, Seattle, Washington* **LETTERER** *Bruce Hale, Seattle, Washington* **TYPOGRAPHIC**
SUPPLIER *Thomas & Kennedy* **STUDIO** *Hornall Anderson Design Works* **CLIENT** *Tree Top, Inc.* **PRINCIPAL TYPES** *MH Madison*
Condensed (text) and Helvetica Packed (capital letters and captions) **DIMENSIONS** *8½ × 11 in. (21.6 × 27.9 cm).*

$7.50

NORMAL

Eco on Calvino

The Virgin in Yugoslavia

Baghdad/Shanghai

Burning Houses

Jasper Johns

Beirut Under Siege

Robert Mapplethorpe

The Princess Who Fell in Love With the Slave

Conversation with Goya

BLACKSTONE

MAGAZINE
TYPOGRAPHY/DESIGN *Paul Davis, José Conde, and Jeanine Esposito, New York, New York* **TYPOGRAPHIC SUPPLIER** *Dynographics Inc.*
STUDIO *Paul Davis Studio* **CLIENT** *Normal Inc.* **PRINCIPAL TYPES** *Various* **DIMENSIONS** *9½ × 13 in. (24.1 × 33 cm).*

POSTER

TYPOGRAPHY/DESIGN *Minoru Niijima and Chiaki Aiba, Setagaya-ku, Tokyo, Japan* **TYPOGRAPHIC SUPPLIER** *Robundo*
STUDIO *Minoru Niijima Design Studio* **CLIENT** *Robundo* **PRINCIPAL TYPES** *Univers 55 and Ryobi Mizui Now Medium*
DIMENSIONS *36 × 23½ in. (91 × 59.4 cm).*

POSTER
TYPOGRAPHY/DESIGN *Cheryl Brzezinski, Houston, Texas* **TYPOGRAPHIC SUPPLIER** *Superior* **STUDIO** *Design Center, Western Michigan University* **CLIENT** *Western Michigan University* **PRINCIPAL TYPE** *Univers 57* **DIMENSIONS** *18 × 24 in. (45.7 × 61 cm).*

With Compliments

Nickeloid
Computer Graphics
Limited

268-282 Waterloo Road
London SE1 8RQ

Telephone 01 928 3053
Telex 266727
Fax 01 261 9625

Nickeloid
Computer Graphics
Limited

268-282 Waterloo Road
London SE1 8RQ

Telephone 01 928 3053
Telex 266727
Fax 01 261 9625

J. J. Smallwood
Managing Director

Nickeloid
Computer Graphics
Limited

268-282 Waterloo Road
London SE1 8RQ
Telephone 01 928 3053
Telex 266727
Fax 01 261 9625

Registered Office
268-282 Waterloo Road
London SE1 8RQ

Registered Number
390573 England

Member of
BPCC Printing
Corporation PLC

STATIONERY
TYPOGRAPHY/DESIGN *David Quay, London, England* **LETTERER** *Paul Gray, London, England* **TYPOGRAPHIC SUPPLIER** *Span Graphics Ltd.*
STUDIO *Quay & Gray Design Consultants* **CLIENT** *Nickeloid Computer Graphics* **PRINCIPAL TYPE** *Galliard Light and Bold*
DIMENSIONS *8½ × 11¾ in. (21 × 29.7 cm).*

LOGOTYPE
TYPOGRAPHY/DESIGN *David Quay, London, England* **LETTERER** *Paul Gray* **STUDIO** *Quay & Gray Design Consultants*
CLIENT *Adplates Group.*

LOGOTYPE
TYPOGRAPHY/DESIGN *Barbara Shimkus, San Antonio, Texas* **CALLIGRAPHERS** *Heeyoung S. Kimm and Barbara Shimkus,*
San Antonio, Texas **STUDIO** *Shimkus Design* **CLIENT** *Dan Wigodsky, San Antonio Museum Association*
PRINCIPAL TYPE *Handlettering.*

POSTER
CREATIVE DIRECTOR *Robin Sweet, New York, New York* **ART DIRECTOR** *Diana Howard* **ILLUSTRATOR** *Rodger Duncan*
TYPOGRAPHIC SUPPLIER *Photo-Lettering, Inc.* **AGENCY** *Vogue Promotion* **CLIENT** *Vogue Advertising* **PRINCIPAL TYPE** *Bauer Bodoni*
DIMENSIONS *19¼ × 32½ in. (48.9 × 82.6 cm).*

MAGAZINE
TYPOGRAPHY/DESIGN *Robert Best, Josh Gosfield, Rhonda Rubenstein, and David Walters, New York, New York*
TYPOGRAPHIC SUPPLIER *In-house* **CLIENT** *New York magazine* **PRINCIPAL TYPES** *Gill Sans Extra Bold Condensed with Hairline*
DIMENSIONS *8³⁄₈ × 10⁷⁄₈ (20.8 × 27.4 cm).*

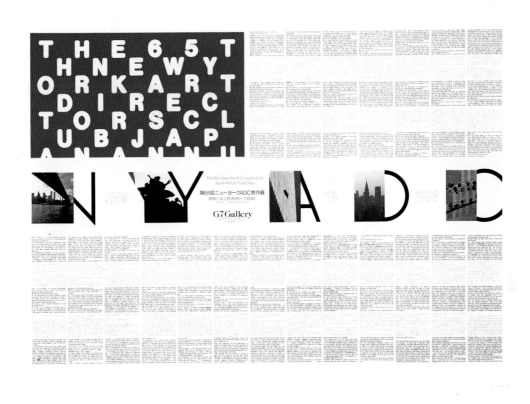

POSTER
TYPOGRAPHY/DESIGN *Masuteru Aoba, Chuo-Ku, Tokyo, Japan* **TYPOGRAPHIC SUPPLIER** *Shakken* **STUDIO** *A & A* **CLIENT** *Recruit Co., Ltd.*
PRINCIPAL TYPE *Mincho* **DIMENSIONS** *57³⁄₈ × 40¹⁄₂ in. (145.6 × 103 cm).*

Commemorating the Bicentennial of the U.S. Constitution 1787–1987

POSTER
TYPOGRAPHY/DESIGN *Saul Bass and Art Goodman, Los Angeles, California* **CALLIGRAPHER** *Saul Bass* **TYPOGRAPHIC**
SUPPLIER *Headliners* **AGENCY** *Saul Bass/Herb Yager and Associates* **STUDIO** *Bass/Yager and Associates* **CLIENT** *Friends of*
Independence National Historic Park **PRINCIPAL TYPE** *Helvetica Bold* **DIMENSIONS** *24 × 32 in. (61 × 81.3 cm).*

POSTER
TYPOGRAPHY/DESIGN *Martha Carothers, Newark, Delaware* **TYPOGRAPHIC SUPPLIER** *Points and Picas* **STUDIO** *The Post Press*
CLIENT *Delaware Heritage Commission* **PRINCIPAL TYPE** *Times Roman Bold* **DIMENSIONS** *36 × 22 in. (91.4 × 55.9 cm).*

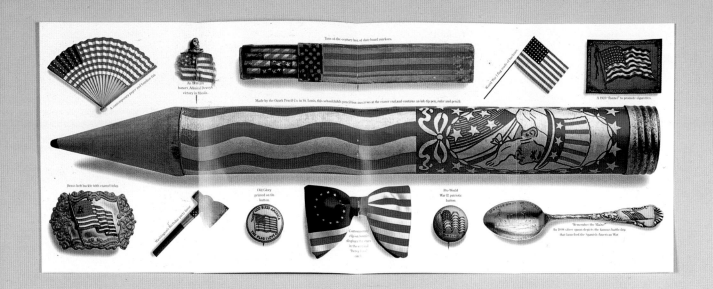

BOOK
TYPOGRAPHY/DESIGN *Kit Hinrichs, San Francisco, California* **TYPOGRAPHIC SUPPLIER** *Reardon & Krebs* **STUDIO** *Pentagram*
CLIENT *Pentagram* **PRINCIPAL TYPE** *Century Old Style* **DIMENSIONS** *5³⁄₄ × 8¹⁄₄ in. (14.6 × 21 cm).*

POSTER

TYPOGRAPHY/DESIGN *Michael Ostro and Susan Rubinroit, Avon, Connecticut* **TYPOGRAPHIC SUPPLIER** *Allied Typesetting*
AGENCY *The Douglas Group, Inc.* **STUDIO** *The Douglas Group, Inc.* **CLIENT** *Riverfront Recapture, Inc.*
PRINCIPAL TYPES *Torino and Trade Gothic Bold Extended* **DIMENSIONS** *12 × 31 in. (30.5 × 78.7 cm).*

POSTER
TYPOGRAPHY/DESIGN *Kit Hinrichs, San Francisco, California* **TYPOGRAPHIC SUPPLIER** *Reardon & Krebs* **STUDIO** *Pentagram*
CLIENT *Computerland* **PRINCIPAL TYPES** *Centaur (text) and Onyx (heads)* **DIMENSIONS** *24 × 36 in. (61 × 91.4 cm).*

CORPORATE IDENTITY
TYPOGRAPHY/DESIGN *Greg Samata and Jim Hardy, Dundee, Illinois* **CALLIGRAPHER** *Susan Mechnig, Dundee, Illinois*
TYPOGRAPHIC SUPPLIER *RyderTypes* **STUDIO** *Samata Associates* **CLIENT** *Rayovac Corporation* **DIMENSIONS** *8½ × 5 in. (22 × 12.7 cm).*

LOGOTYPE
TYPOGRAPHY/DESIGN *Emilio V. Brunetti, Astoria, New York* **LETTERER** *Emilio V. Brunetti* **STUDIO** *Brunetti Design Studio*
CLIENT *Exploding Rhythm* **PRINCIPAL TYPE** *Helvetica Medium.*

LOGOTYPE
TYPOGRAPHY/DESIGN *Oswaldo Miranda (Miran), Curitiba, PR, Brazil* **CALLIGRAPHER** *Oswaldo Miranda (Miran)*
TYPOGRAPHIC SUPPLIER *Digital* **STUDIO** *Módulo 3* **CLIENT** *Módulo 3.*

EDITORIAL
TYPOGRAPHY/DESIGN *Oswaldo Miranda (Miran), Curitiba, PR, Brazil* **CALLIGRAPHER** *Oswaldo Miranda (Miran)*
TYPOGRAPHIC SUPPLIER *Digital* **STUDIO** *Módulo 3* **CLIENT** *Revista Grafica* **DIMENSIONS** *10½ × 20 in. (26.7 × 50.8 cm).*

59

THE CONCEPT THAT CREATED A SCHOOL.

LOGOTYPE
TYPOGRAPHY/DESIGN *Dan Liew, San Francisco, California* **CALLIGRAPHER** *Dan Liew* **TYPOGRAPHIC SUPPLIER** *AdCom* **AGENCY** *AdCom*
CLIENT *Academy of Art College* **PRINCIPAL TYPE** *Novarese.*

BOTH SIDES.
IDEAS FROM
LOOKING AT
OR REQUIRE
MAY ALLOW

Philosophy

IS A SCIENCE
DEFINED AS
THE PURSUIT,
STUDY & LOVE
OF WISDOM.

SELF-PROMOTION
TYPOGRAPHY/DESIGN *John Langdon, Wenonah, New Jersey* **LETTERER** *John Langdon* **TYPOGRAPHIC SUPPLIER** *Armstrong Typography*
STUDIO *John Langdon Design* **CLIENT** *John Langdon Design* **PRINCIPAL TYPES** *Handlettering and Avant Garde Gothic Extra Light*
DIMENSIONS *8½ × 11 in. (21.6 × 27.9 cm).*

STATIONERY
TYPOGRAPHY/DESIGN *Andrew Kramer, New York, New York* **LETTERER** *Andrew Kramer* **TYPOGRAPHIC SUPPLIER** *The Graphic Word, Inc.*
AGENCY *Kramer Associates, Inc.* **CLIENT** *Shoe Biz* **PRINCIPAL TYPE** *Novarese* **DIMENSIONS** *8½ × 11 in. (21.6 × 27.9 cm).*

BOOK
TYPOGRAPHY/DESIGN *Erwin Fieger, Castelfranco di Sopra, Italy* **CALLIGRAPHER** *Erwin Fieger* **CLIENT** *Harenberg Kommunikation*
DIMENSIONS *4³⁄₄ × 6⁷⁄₈ in. (12 × 17.5 cm).*

LOGOTYPE
TYPOGRAPHY/DESIGN *Peter Lord, New York, New York* **LETTERER** *Peter Lord* **CLIENT** *Peter Lord.*

A master chef is not easily pleased.  He neither knows, nor cares, that you protect your apples from codling moths and apple maggots longer with ®GUTHION insecticide. Or that GUTHION is gentle on desirable predator mites. He only knows that your apples are unblemished. Beautiful. And worthy of being showcased in one of his creations. Maybe that's why GUTHION has been the choice of apple growers like you for three decades. Because come harvest time, you know you'll get your just desserts.

GUTHION

Mobay Corporation, Agricultural Chemicals Division, Box 4913, Kansas City, MO 64120
GUTHION is a Reg. TM of Bayer AG, Leverkusen.   87103

ADVERTISEMENT
TYPOGRAPHY/DESIGN *Skye Hyers, Kansas City, Missouri* CALLIGRAPHER *Aaron Presler, Kansas City, Missouri* TYPOGRAPHIC SUPPLIER *Uppercase* AGENCY *Valentine/Radford Advertising* STUDIO *Partners, Inc.* CLIENT *Guthion Mobay Corporation* PRINCIPAL TYPE *Weidemann* DIMENSIONS *10½ × 13½ in. (26.7 × 34.3 cm).*

LABEL
TYPOGRAPHY/DESIGN *Tim Girvin and Peg Ogle, Seattle, Washington* **CALLIGRAPHERS** *Tim Girvin and Anton Kimball*
TYPOGRAPHIC SUPPLIER *Thomas & Kennedy* **STUDIO** *Tim Girvin Design* **CLIENT** *Salmon Bay Wine* **PRINCIPAL TYPE** *Handlettering.*

POSTER

TYPOGRAPHY/DESIGN *Robert Horn and Daniel Goodenough, Chicago, Illinois* **ART DIRECTORS** *Robert Horn and Gary Alfredson, Chicago, Illinois* **LETTERER** *Robert Horn* **TYPOGRAPHIC SUPPLIER** *Prototype* C.A.D. **STUDIO** *Robert Horn Design Ensemble* **CLIENT** *The New Chicago Coalition* **PRINCIPAL TYPES** *Handlettering and Bauer Text* **DIMENSIONS** *17 × 25½ in. (48.2 × 64.8 cm).*

ASSOCIATION
of AMERICAN
COLLEGES

1818 R Street, N.W.
Washington, D.C.
20009

202/387-3760

THE VOICE
for LIBERAL
LEARNING

ASSOCIATION
of AMERICAN
COLLEGES

1818 R Street, N.W.
Washington, D.C.
20009
202/387-3760

SHERRY LEVY-REINER
Director of Public Information
and Publications

STATIONERY
TYPOGRAPHY/DESIGN *Liz Clark, Baltimore, Maryland* **CALLIGRAPHER** *Wil Davidson, Philadelphia, Pennsylvania*
TYPOGRAPHIC SUPPLIER *Alpha Graphics* **STUDIO** *North Charles Street Design* **CLIENT** *Association of American Colleges*
PRINCIPAL TYPES *Goudy and handlettering* **DIMENSIONS** *8½ × 11 in. (21.6 × 27.9 cm).*

Sixty calligraphic renderings of Bible passages with notes by the artist

Timothy R. Botts

BOOK
TYPOGRAPHY/DESIGN *Timothy R. Botts and Glen Ellyn, Illinois* **CALLIGRAPHER** *Timothy R. Botts* **TYPOGRAPHIC SUPPLIER** *Ameritype*
CLIENT *Tyndale House Publishers* **PRINCIPAL TYPE** *Diotima* **DIMENSIONS** *8½ × 11 in. (21.6 × 27.9 cm).*

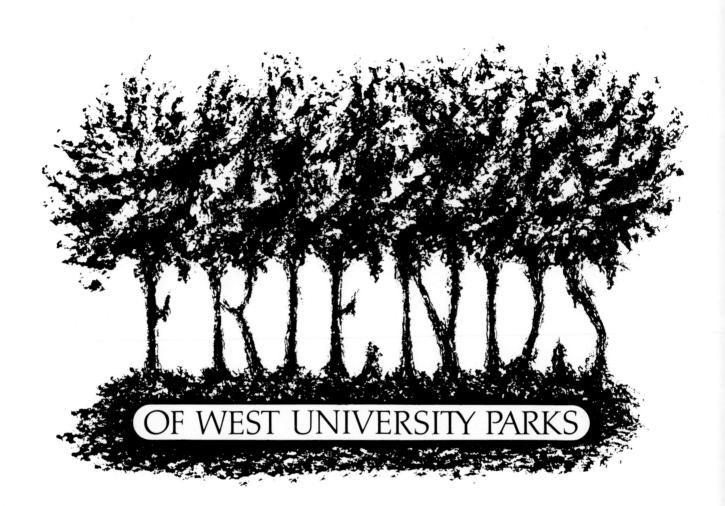

LOGOTYPE
TYPOGRAPHY/DESIGN *Richard High, Houston, Texas* **LETTERER** *Richard High* **STUDIO** *Richard High Design* **CLIENT** *Friends of West University Parks* **PRINCIPAL TYPE** *Palatino.*

BOASE MASSIMI POLLITT plc

Annual Report & Accounts 1985

ANNUAL REPORT
TYPOGRAPHY/DESIGN *Jackie Vicary, London, England* **CALLIGRAPHER** *Kira Josey, Surrey, England* **TYPOGRAPHIC SUPPLIER** *Wordwork*
AGENCY *Michael Peters Group* **STUDIO** *Michael Peters Literature Limited* **CLIENT** *Boase Massimi Pollitt PLC* **PRINCIPAL TYPES** *Plantin*
(text) and Bodoni (headings) **DIMENSIONS** *8¹/₄ × 11³/₄ in. (21 × 29.7 cm).*

BOOK
TYPOGRAPHY/DESIGN *Paula Scher, New York, New York* **TYPOGRAPHIC SUPPLIER** *Personal collection of Paula Scher*
STUDIO *Koppel & Scher* **CLIENT** *Simon & Schuster* **PRINCIPAL TYPE** *Berlina* **DIMENSIONS** *4 × 5 in. (10.2 × 12.7 cm).*

Crater to the Olduvai Gorge itself and there, from a deep crack in the basalt, he pulled out an old, old chest. When the Old Barman of the Ngorongoro Hilton finally managed to open the chest, Froud saw, to his amazement, that it contained no less than forty-three dusty, mouldering notebooks—the exact number of cases of Chevalier-Montrachet he had left! To his even greater astonishment, each notebook proved to be packed with sketches and lightning portraits of all the goblins who inhabited the Labyrinth in those long vanished times.

Froud instantly gave up mucepodunry (which wasn't all that hard to do) and devoted the rest of his sober moments to studying this cornucopia of ancient goblin portraiture.

The goblin artist, whose work had been so miraculously preserved, appears to have been a certain Diabe! His technique was quick and direct, but unfortunately his concentration was less than satisfactory, and many of the 'portraits' consisted of but a few lines thrown down apparently randomly on the page. However, after years of study and hardly any flower-arranging, Froud was able to compare and cross-reference the lines and fragments so as to build up fuller likenesses of the goblins portrayed. At length (i.e., 70 cases of Savigny-Lès-Beaune, 12 Ladoix, 46 Nuits-St-Georges, 27 Romanée-Conti, 65 Vosne-Romanée, 54 Chabolle-Musigny and 435 Chablis) Froud was even able to reconstruct their names.

This book is the result of all that wine-and-study, and represents the fullest record yet discovered of the Goblins of the Labyrinth.

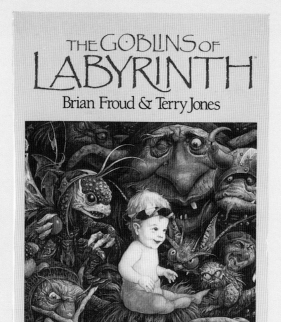

BOOK
TYPOGRAPHY/DESIGN *Marc Cheshire, New York, New York* **TYPOGRAPHIC SUPPLIER** *Trufont Typographers, Inc.* **CLIENT** *Henry Holt and Company* **PRINCIPAL TYPE** *ITC Berkeley Old Style* **DIMENSIONS** *9 × 12 in. (22.9 × 30.5 cm).*

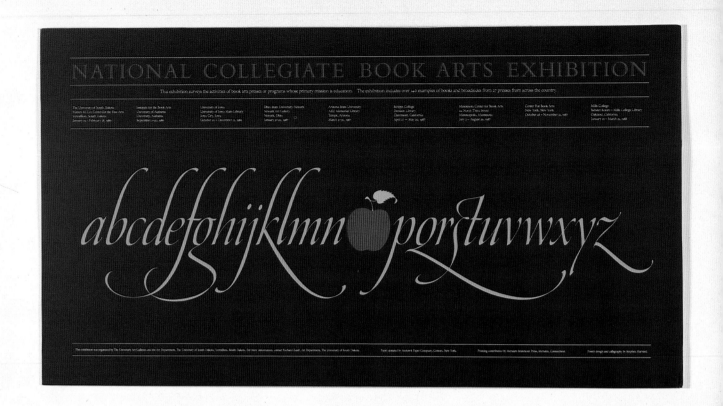

POSTER
TYPOGRAPHY/DESIGN *Stephen Harvard, Lunenburg, Vermont* **CALLIGRAPHER** *Stephen Harvard* **TYPOGRAPHIC SUPPLIER** *Meriden-Stinehour Press* **CLIENT** *National Collegiate Book Arts Exhibition* **DIMENSIONS** *36 × 19½ in. (91.4 × 49.5 cm).*

Grand opera requires the marshalling of enormous forces, both human and financial. The commitment is great; the benefits are even greater. As an organization of international renown, The Dallas Opera reflects great credit on our city. To increase its prominence, it must continue to reach for new heights. Thus we have embarked upon a program of support as grand and sweeping as any operatic production --

The Landmark Campaign

David Donosky
Chairman, Landmark Campaign

BOOK
TYPOGRAPHY/DESIGN *Chuck Hart, St. Louis, Missouri, and Bob Young, Dallas, Texas* **CALLIGRAPHER** *Aaron Presler, Kansas City, Missouri* **TYPOGRAPHIC SUPPLIER** *Robert J. Hilton Co., Inc.* **AGENCY** *Krause & Young* **STUDIO** *Partners, Inc.* **CLIENT** *The Dallas Opera* **PRINCIPAL TYPE** *Bodoni* **DIMENSIONS** *9¼ × 12³/₁₆ in. (23.5 × 30.9 cm).*

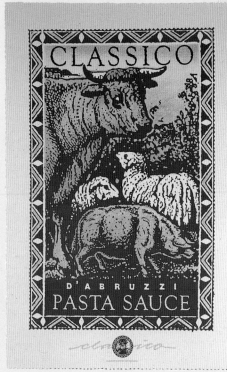

CAMPAIGN POSTERS
TYPOGRAPHY/DESIGN *Charles Spencer Anderson, Minneapolis, Minnesota* **TYPOGRAPHIC SUPPLIER** *Typeshooters*
STUDIO *Duffy Design Group* **CLIENT** *Prince Foods (Classico)* **PRINCIPAL TYPE** *Goudy (customized)*
DIMENSIONS *28 × 18¾ in. (71.1 × 47.6 cm).*

POSTERS
TYPOGRAPHY/DESIGN *Bryan L. Peterson, Dallas, Texas* **LETTERER** *Bryan L. Peterson* **TYPOGRAPHIC SUPPLIER** *Typeworks*
STUDIO *SMU Publications Services* **CLIENT** *Southern Methodist University* **PRINCIPAL TYPE** *Galliard*
DIMENSIONS *12 × 25 in. (30.5 × 63.5 cm).*

CAMPAIGN
TYPOGRAPHY/DESIGN *Barry Slavin, Carol Neiger, and Jim Hutchison, Chicago, Illinois* **CALLIGRAPHER** *John Weber, Glenview, Illinois*
TYPOGRAPHIC SUPPLIER *Typesmiths* **STUDIO** *Slavin Associates, Inc.* **CLIENT** *Windward Associates Limited Partnership*
PRINCIPAL TYPES *Goudy Handtooled and Janson* **DIMENSIONS** *9 × 12 in. (22.9 × 30.2 cm).*

FOLIO COVER
TYPOGRAPHY/DESIGN *JoAnne Bohannon, Seattle, Washington* **CALLIGRAPHER** *Iskra Johnson, Seattle, Washington*
ILLUSTRATOR *Jim Hays, Marysville, Washington* **TYPOGRAPHIC SUPPLIER** *Thomas & Kennedy* **AGENCY** *Evans Kraft*
CLIENT *California Artichoke Advisory Board* **DIMENSIONS** *9 × 12 in. (22.7 × 30.3 cm).*

YOU HAVE JUST experienced the most remarkable breakthrough in type since the development of digital typesetting technology. The large letter *Y* shown, has been faithfully reproduced from actual sized, unretouched output of the CG 9600 imagesetter. The 9600 from Compugraphic Corporation utilizes CG LaserType,™ a unique curvilinear database that provides superior quality type output in sizes ranging from 4 to 999 points. ¶As you can see from the cleanness of the edges and the smoothness of the curves, CG LaserType reproduces typefaces with true fidelity to the original design. Every type character is produced by true arc outline data rather than vectors, resulting in exceptionally smooth contours, sharper corners and straighter lines than previous digital systems; no more jagged or stair-step edges on the type.

Cg compugraphic®

ADVERTISEMENT
TYPOGRAPHY/DESIGN *Susan Darbyshire, Joseph Hannaford, and Mark Holden, Wilmington, Massachusetts*
TYPOGRAPHIC SUPPLIER *Compugraphic Corporation* **AGENCY** *Compugraphic Corporation (in-house)* **CLIENT** *Compugraphic Type Division*
PRINCIPAL TYPES *VGC Egyptian 505 and Flemish Script II* **DIMENSIONS** *10 × 13½ in. (25.4 × 34.3 cm).*

On a job this big, others may

run you a little ragged.

Not Thompson Type.

We're big on Quality.

ThompsonType
619·224·3137

BASKERVILLE

81

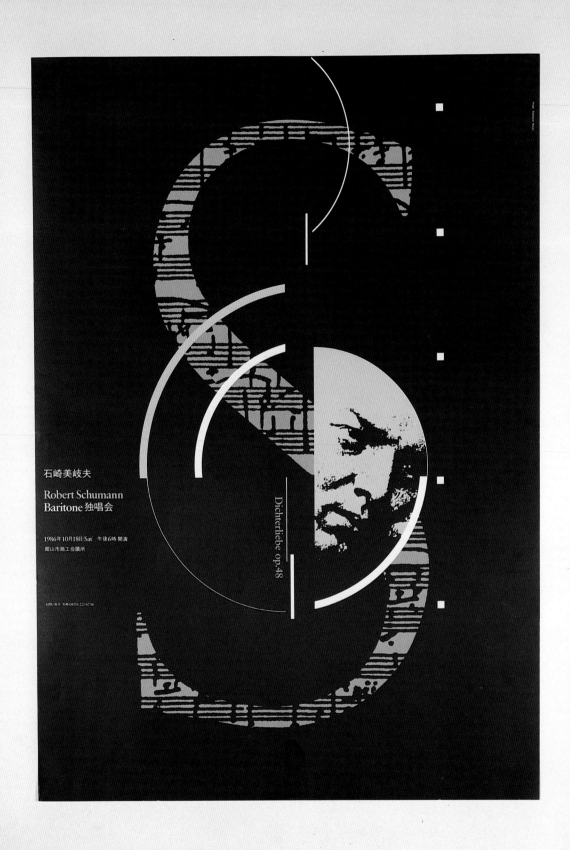

POSTER

TYPOGRAPHY/DESIGN *Masato Tsukamoto, Setagaya-ku, Tokyo, Japan* **TYPOGRAPHIC SUPPLIER** *Robundo* **AGENCY** *Azusa Planning*
STUDIO *Masato Tsukamoto Design Studio* **CLIENT** *Azusa Planning* **PRINCIPAL TYPES** *Shakken DC-KL and Sabon Antiqua*
DIMENSIONS $28\,5/8 \times 20\,1/4\,in.$ *(72.8 × 51.5 cm).*

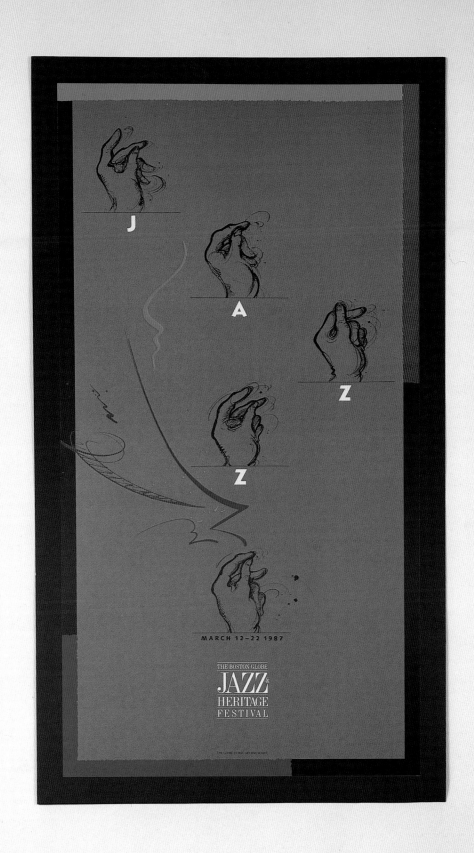

POSTER
TYPOGRAPHY/DESIGN *John Avery, Boston, Massachusetts* **TYPOGRAPHIC SUPPLIER** *Wrightson Typography* **AGENCY** *Hill, Holliday/Design*
CLIENT *The Boston Globe* **PRINCIPAL TYPE** *Grizzly* **DIMENSIONS** *14 × 26 in. (35.5 × 66 cm).*

POSTER
TYPOGRAPHY/DESIGN *Joe Duffy, Minneapolis, Minnesota* **TYPOGRAPHIC SUPPLIER** *Typeshooters* **STUDIO** *Duffy Design Group*
CLIENT *Fallon McElligott* **PRINCIPAL TYPE** *Helvetica Stencil* **DIMENSIONS** *40 × 20½ in. (101.6 × 52.1 cm).*

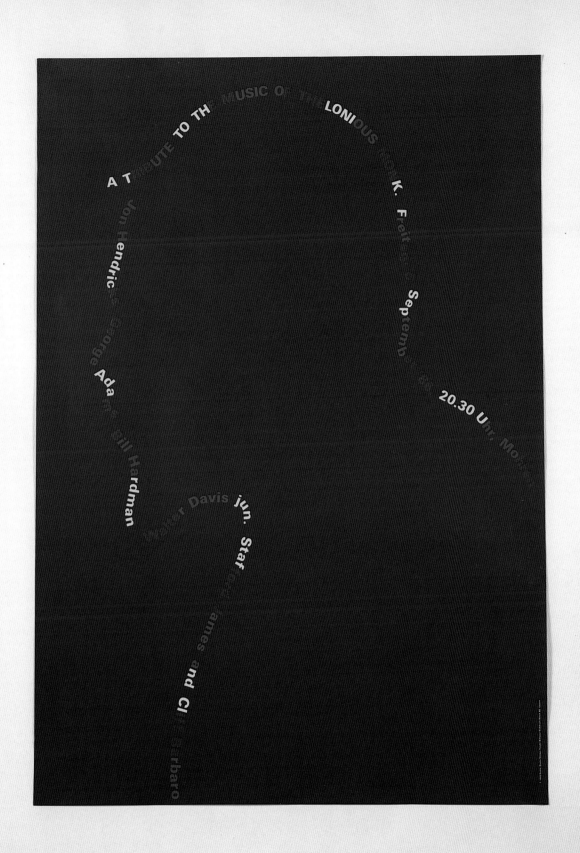

POSTER
TYPOGRAPHY/DESIGN *Niklaus Troxler, Willisau, Switzerland* **LETTERER** *Niklaus Troxler* **TYPOGRAPHIC SUPPLIER** *Layout-Satz AG*
STUDIO *Grafik-Studio Niklaus Troxler* **CLIENT** *Jazz in Willisau* **PRINCIPAL TYPE** *Univers 75 Bold* **DIMENSIONS** *50³/₈ × 35 in.*
(127.9 × 88.9 cm).

伊藤勝一の
漢字の感字
THE IMAGE OF KANJI BY KATSUICHI ITO

BOOK
TYPOGRAPHY/DESIGN *Katsuichi Ito, Minato-ku, Tokyo, Japan* **LETTERER** *Katsuichi Ito* **TYPOGRAPHIC SUPPLIER** *Robundo*
STUDIO *Katsuichi Ito Design Studio* **CLIENT** *Robundo* **PRINCIPAL TYPE** *Shakken MM-OKL* **DIMENSIONS** *7⅝ × 9½ in. (19.4 × 24.1 cm).*

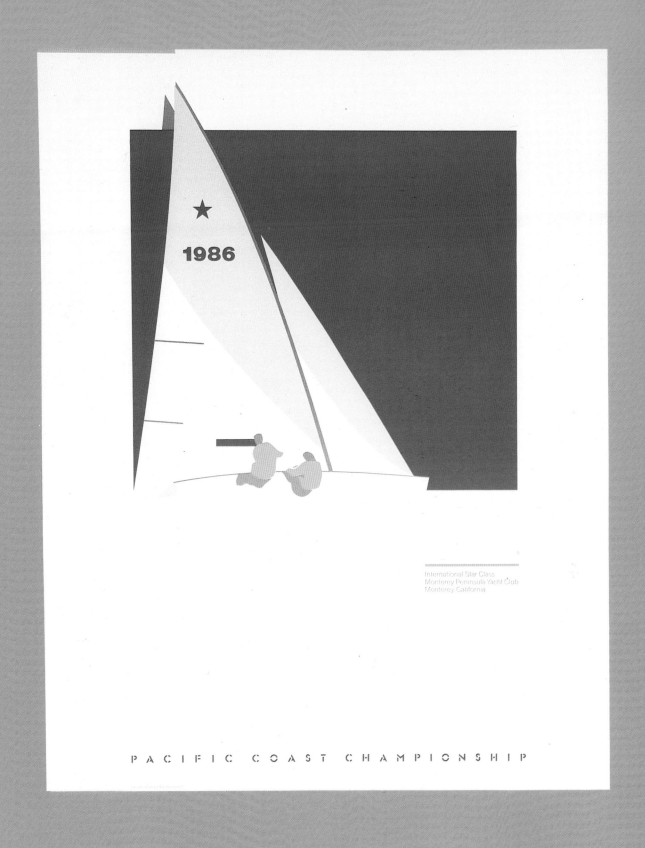

POSTER
TYPOGRAPHY/DESIGN *Jonelle Woolward, San Francisco, California* **TYPOGRAPHIC SUPPLIER** *Mercury Typography, Inc.*
AGENCY *Woolward & Company* **CLIENT** *Monterey Peninsula Yacht Club* **PRINCIPAL TYPE** *Stencil Bold* **DIMENSIONS** *16 × 20 in.*
(40.6 × 50.8 cm).

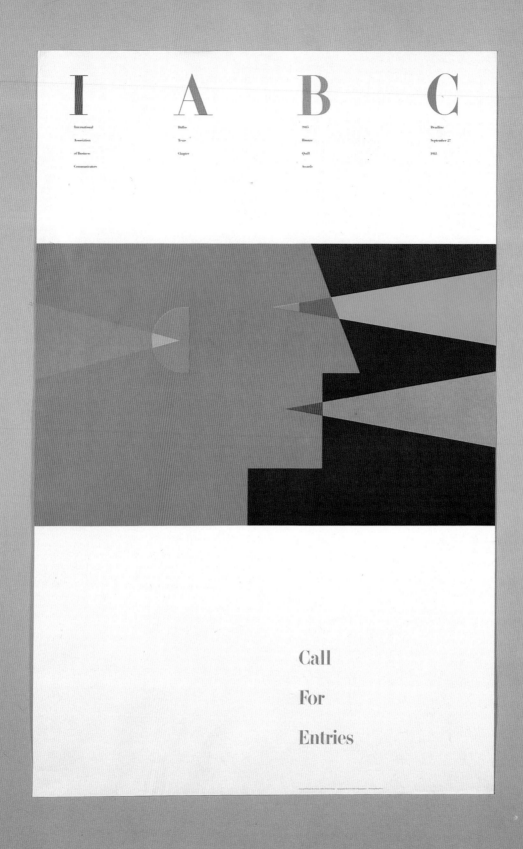

POSTER
TYPOGRAPHY/DESIGN *Don Sibley, Dallas, Texas* **TYPOGRAPHIC SUPPLIER** *Southwestern Typographics* **STUDIO** *Sibley/Peteet Design, Inc.*
CLIENT *International Association of Business Communicators (IABC)* **PRINCIPAL TYPES** *Bauer Bodoni and Bodoni Book*
DIMENSIONS *37 × 22½ in. (94 × 56.4 cm).*

BROCHURE

TYPOGRAPHY/DESIGN *Pascale Werckshagen, Offenbach am Main, West Germany* LETTERER *Alexander Branczyk, Offenbach am Main, West Germany* TYPOGRAPHIC SUPPLIER *Berthold* CLIENT *Berthold* PRINCIPAL TYPE *Concorde Nova* DIMENSIONS *8¹/2 × 11 in. (21 × 29.7 cm).*

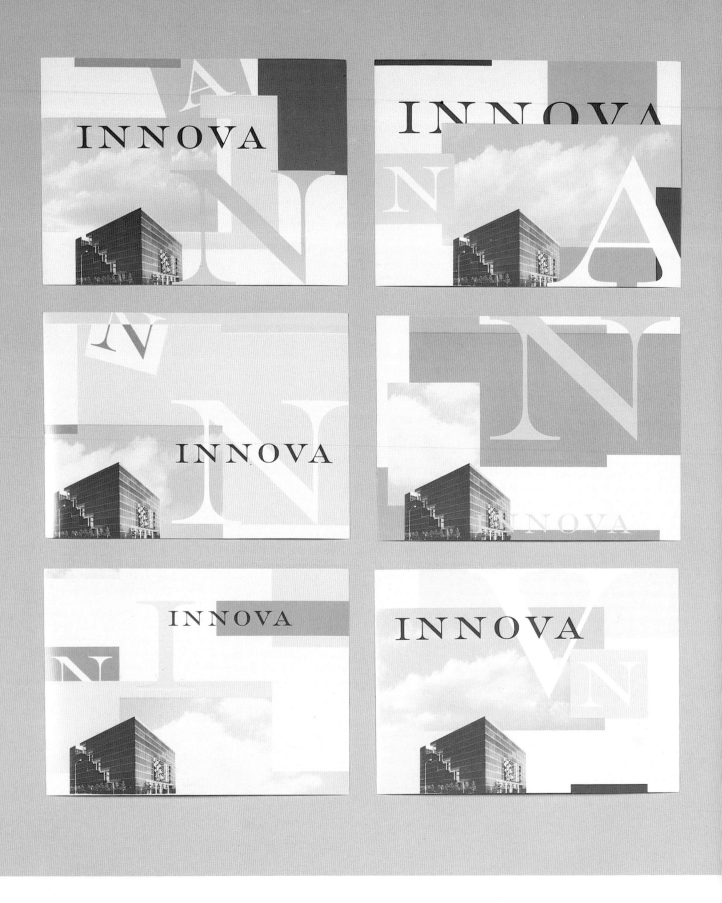

POSTCARD SERIES
TYPOGRAPHY/DESIGN *James P. Williams, Houston, Texas* **TYPOGRAPHIC SUPPLIER** *Characters* **STUDIO** *Creel Morrell Inc.*
CLIENT *Innova* **PRINCIPAL TYPE** *Engravers Roman* **DIMENSIONS** *5 × 7 in. (17.7 × 12.7 cm).*

POSTER
TYPOGRAPHY/DESIGN *Margi Denton and Barbara Cooper, Pasadena, California* **TYPOGRAPHIC SUPPLIER** *Alpha Graphix and Central Typesetting* **STUDIO** *Denton Design Associates* **CLIENT** *California Institute of Technology* **PRINCIPAL TYPE** *Garamond* **DIMENSIONS** *36 × 24 in. (91.4 × 61 cm).*

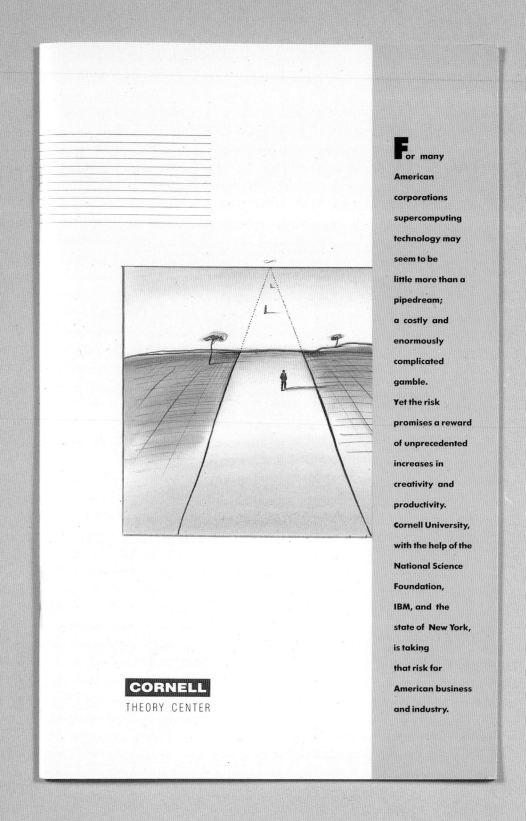

For many American corporations supercomputing technology may seem to be little more than a pipedream; a costly and enormously complicated gamble. Yet the risk promises a reward of unprecedented increases in creativity and productivity. Cornell University, with the help of the National Science Foundation, IBM, and the state of New York, is taking that risk for American business and industry.

BROCHURE
TYPOGRAPHY/DESIGN *Fausto Pellegrini and Nadia Pignatone, New York, New York* **TYPOGRAPHIC SUPPLIER** *Typologic*
AGENCY *Jan Krukowski Associates* **CLIENT** *Cornell University* **PRINCIPAL TYPE** *Futura* **DIMENSIONS** *8½ × 11 in. (21.6 × 27.9 cm).*

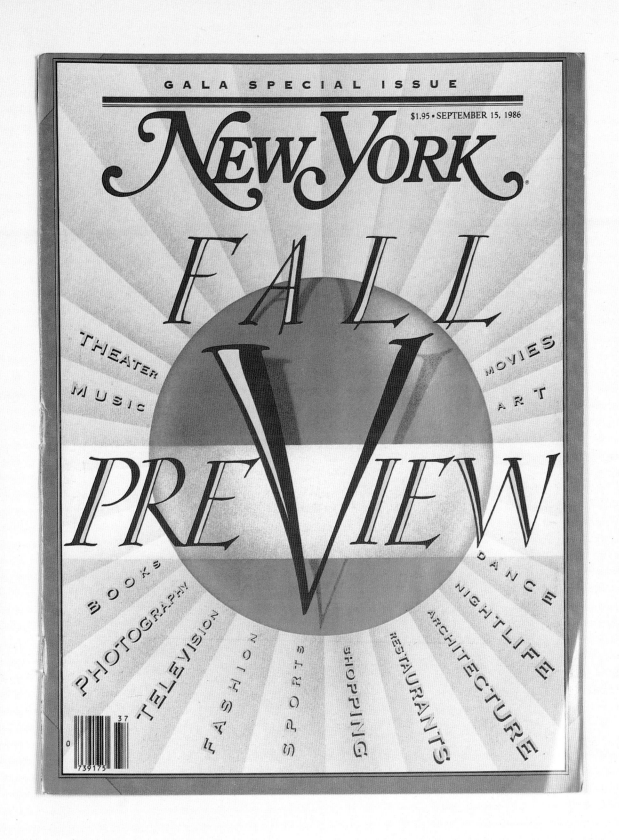

MAGAZINE
TYPOGRAPHY/DESIGN *Robert Best, New York, New York* ARTIST *Fred Swanson* TYPOGRAPHIC SUPPLIER *Solo Type*
CLIENT *New York magazine* PRINCIPAL TYPE *Eve Light Italic* DIMENSIONS *8³/₁₆ × 10⁷/₈ in. (20.8 × 27.4 cm).*

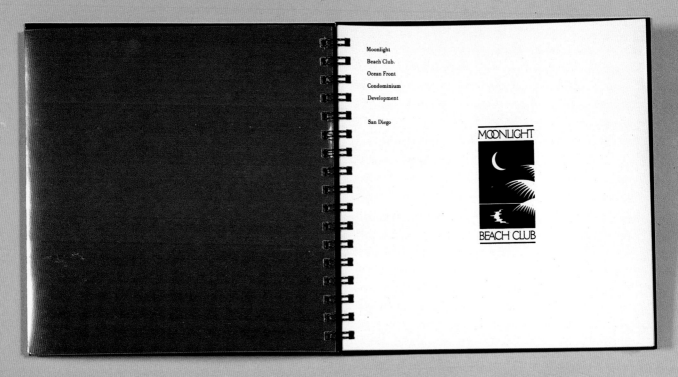

Moonlight
Beach Club.
Ocean Front
Condominium
Development

San Diego

BOOK
TYPOGRAPHY/DESIGN *Rex Peteet and Judy Dolim, Dallas, Texas* **TYPOGRAPHIC SUPPLIER** *Robert J. Hilton Co., Inc.*
STUDIO *Sibley/Peteet Design, Inc.* **CLIENT** *Sibley/Peteet Design, Inc.* **PRINCIPAL TYPE** *Bodoni* **DIMENSIONS** *6 × 6 in. (15.2 × 15.2 cm).*

BROCHURE
TYPOGRAPHY/DESIGN *Steven Tolleson and Susan Gross, San Francisco, California* **TYPOGRAPHIC SUPPLIER** *Spartan Typographers*
STUDIO *Tolleson Design* **CLIENT** *The National Press* **PRINCIPAL TYPES** *Futura Bold, Garamond Italic, Gill Sans Condensed, Modern No. 216, ITC Heavy and Light Italic, and Perpetua* **DIMENSIONS** *7½ × 10⅞ in. (19.2 × 27.7 cm).*

TOYS IN THE ATTIC

TOYS IN THE ATTIC

WITH COMPLIMENTS

29 GREAT QUEEN STREET, COVENT GARDEN, LONDON WC2E 7AB. TELEPHONE 01-405 4865

TOYS IN THE ATTIC

ANDY HILL
(THE BOSS)

29 GREAT QUEEN STREET, COVENT GARDEN, LONDON WC2E 7AB. TELEPHONE 01-405 4865

29 GREAT QUEEN STREET, COVENT GARDEN, LONDON WC2E 7AB. TELEPHONE 01-405 4865
DIRECTORS: ANDY HILL, ROB ISTED. V.A.T.No: 429 5428 31. REGISTERED IN ENGLAND 1912373

STATIONERY
TYPOGRAPHY/DESIGN *Paul Gray, London, England* **LETTERER** *Paul Gray* **TYPOGRAPHIC SUPPLIER** *Span Graphics Ltd.*
STUDIO *Quay & Gray Design Consultants* **CLIENT** *Toys in The Attic* **PRINCIPAL TYPE** *Helvetica Light*
DIMENSIONS *8½ × 11¾ in. (21.6 × 29.7 cm).*

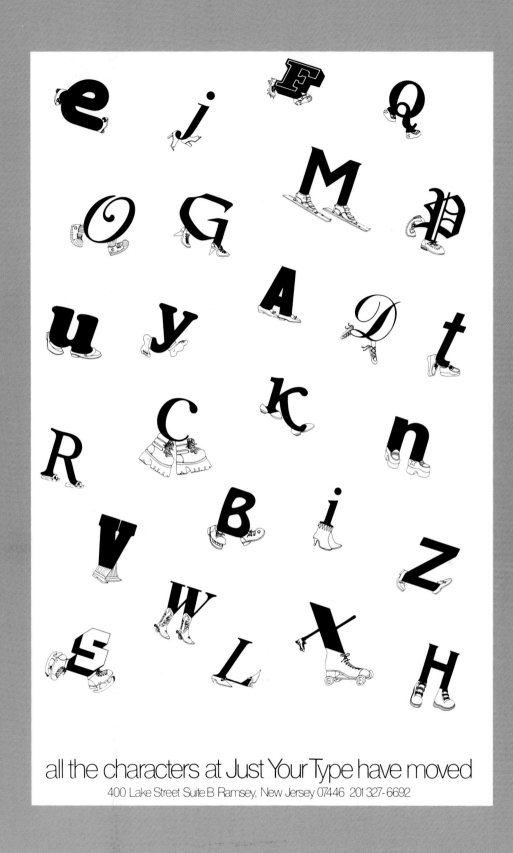

POSTER

TYPOGRAPHY/DESIGN *Arthur Boden, Ramsey, New Jersey* ILLUSTRATOR *Michael Schuetz* TYPOGRAPHIC SUPPLIER *Just Your Type*
AGENCY *Arthur Boden, Inc.* STUDIO *Just Your Type* CLIENT *Arthur Boden, Inc.* PRINCIPAL TYPE *Helvetica Thin*
DIMENSIONS *23 × 35 in. (58.4 × 88.9 cm).*

BROCHURE
TYPOGRAPHY/DESIGN *Buck Smith, St. Louis, Missouri* **CALLIGRAPHER** *Carolyn Goss, St. Louis, Missouri*
TYPOGRAPHIC SUPPLIER *Paragon Typographers, Inc.* **AGENCY** *Bartels & Carstens, Inc.* **CLIENT** *Southwestern Bell Corporation*
PRINCIPAL TYPE *Futura* **DIMENSIONS** *8½ × 5½ in. (21.6 × 13.9 cm).*

François Weil, sans un mot,
donne la parole aux signes.
Il tisse et entrelace, creuse et
évase, plie et tord la matière.
L'arc se tend, la ligne se brise,
mais jamais la forme n'est
agressive. Elle chante.

Son trait épais s'enroule et se
déroule. Graciles, les fibres
vibrent. Les lettres s'effacent,
leurs traces cannevassent.
La forme devient sigle, la forme
vous fait signe.

Même les chiffres s'animent :
le 1, mouvement-ébauche vers
l'infini. Le 4 aspiré par les points
cardinaux ; le 3 et le 5 tout à la
fois hiératiques et entraînants.

Livrez à François Weil votre
entreprise, sa raison sociale,
sa complexité, sa réputation,
ses produits, ses aspirations.
Il prend tout, analyse et globalise.
Et là où converge son
imaginaire, la forme se déploie.
Posée sur le papier, elle
y trouve sa profondeur.
Et par là sa résonnance.

Faites-lui signe pour vos sigles ...

Christine Arfeuillères
Marie-José Protais

sigle pour un colloque sur la petite hydraulique à Sophia-Antipolis.

BROCHURE
TYPOGRAPHY/DESIGN *François Weil, Paris, France* **TYPOGRAPHIC SUPPLIER** *Face Photosetting* **STUDIO** *François Weil*
CLIENT *François Weil* **PRINCIPAL TYPE** *Goudy Old Style* **DIMENSIONS** *12 × 17 in. (30.5 × 43 cm).*

BOOK
TYPOGRAPHY/DESIGN *Steve Gibbs, Dallas, Texas* **LETTERER** *Steve Gibbs* **TYPOGRAPHIC SUPPLIER** *Typographics*
AGENCY *Childs Communications* **STUDIO** *Gibbs Design* **CLIENT** *VMS* **PRINCIPAL TYPE** *Fenice*
DIMENSIONS *10 × 15 in. (25.4 × 38.1 cm).*

Longing for a far-away place where the palm trees and the hula dancers sway? Participate in the VMS Vacation Incentive Program. You'll really go places.

CAMPAIGN
TYPOGRAPHY/DESIGN *Steve Gibbs, Dallas, Texas* **LETTERER** *Steve Gibbs* **TYPOGRAPHIC SUPPLIER** *Typographics*
AGENCY *Childs Communications* **STUDIO** *Gibbs Design* **CLIENT** *VMS* **PRINCIPAL TYPE** *Fenice* **DIMENSIONS** *10 × 15 in. (25.4 × 38.1 cm).*

POSTER

TYPOGRAPHY/DESIGN *Bryan L. Peterson, Dallas, Texas* **TYPOGRAPHIC SUPPLIER** *Typeworks* **STUDIO** *Peterson & Company*
CLIENT *Peterson & Company* **PRINCIPAL TYPE** *Futura Bold Condensed* **DIMENSIONS** *15½ × 34 in. (39.7 × 86.4 cm).*

Merry Christmas from Bauhaus to Your House. Tina, Bruce, Nick, Stephanie, David and Sabu.

POSTER
TYPOGRAPHY/DESIGN *Bruce Blackburn, New York, New York* **LETTERER** *Bruce Blackburn* **TYPOGRAPHIC SUPPLIER** *CT Typografix, Inc.*
STUDIO *Blackburn & Associates* **CLIENT** *The Blackburn Family* **PRINCIPAL TYPE** *Futura Book* **DIMENSIONS** *20 × 25 in. (50 × 62.5 cm).*

POSTER

TYPOGRAPHY/DESIGN *Ken Cato, Melbourne, Victoria, Australia* **CALLIGRAPHER** *Anita Xhaffer, Melbourne, Victoria, Australia*
TYPOGRAPHIC SUPPLIER *Epitype Pty. Ltd.* **AGENCY** *Ken Cato Design Company Pty. Ltd.* **STUDIO** *Ken Cato Design Company Pty. Ltd.*
CLIENT *Australian Type Directors Club* **PRINCIPAL TYPE** *Flyer Bold Condensed* **DIMENSIONS** *24 × 39¼ in. (61 × 99.7 cm).*

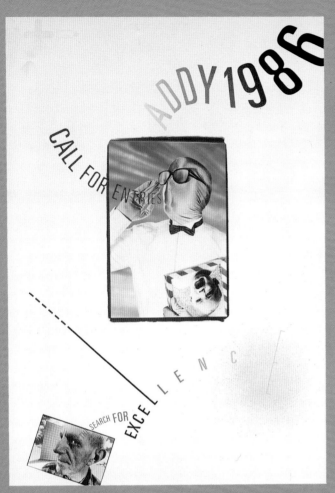

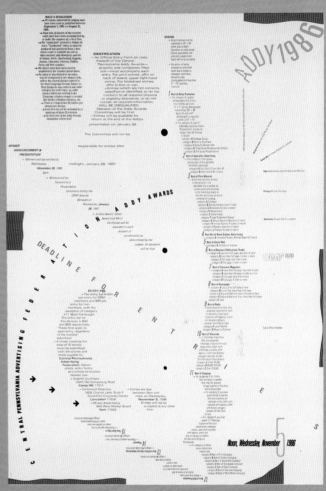

POSTER
TYPOGRAPHY/DESIGN *Jerry King Musser, Harrisburg, Pennsylvania* **LETTERER** *Jerry King Musser* **TYPOGRAPHIC SUPPLIER** *Centennial Graphics, Inc.* **STUDIO** *Musser Design* **CLIENT** *Central Pennsylvania Advertising Federation* **PRINCIPAL TYPE** *Univers* **DIMENSIONS** *19 × 27 in. (48.2 × 68.5 cm).*

REGISTER NOW!

Are you getting out of school and trying to line up a job? Or even better, a career? One that's bright and unlimited. One where you can still work with your hands or work with computers, film, or the latest high tech machines. It pays to look into printing. See your counselor. And sign up today.

POSTER
TYPOGRAPHY/DESIGN *Dick Mitchell, Dallas, Texas* **TYPOGRAPHIC SUPPLIER** *Phil's Phototype* **AGENCY** *The Richards Group*
STUDIO *Richards Brock Miller Mitchell and Associates* **CLIENT** *Printing Industries Association* **PRINCIPAL TYPE** *Trade Gothic Bold Condensed* **DIMENSIONS** *29³/₁₆ × 20 in. (74.8 × 51.3 cm).*

BROCHURE
TYPOGRAPHY/DESIGN *Ken Cooke and Eric Scott, New York, New York* **TYPOGRAPHIC SUPPLIER** *Typogram* **AGENCY** *Identica, Inc.*
CLIENT *Fisher Camuto Group* **PRINCIPAL TYPE** *Futura Extra Bold* **DIMENSIONS** *8½×11 in. (21.6×27.9 cm).*

CORPORATE IDENTITY
TYPOGRAPHY/DESIGN *Richard Rogers and David Scott, New York, New York* **TYPOGRAPHIC SUPPLIER** *Grid Typographic Services Inc.*
AGENCY *Richard Rogers Inc.* **STUDIO** *Richard Rogers Inc.* **CLIENT** *Grid Typographic Services Inc.* **PRINCIPAL TYPE** *Bodoni*
DIMENSIONS *Various.*

FORM NO 1

TRANSFORMERS

A Transformer is based on a 'source' Data Map and a 'target' Data Map. It is always associated with subfile generation, and specifies how a parent-file record is to be 'transformed' into the subfile's record. If a Transformer is NOT specified, the subfile record is exactly the same as the parent-file record; a Transformer would be used to extract and compress only selected data into a smaller record. The output Data Map may call for a field to be stored in a different format than it appears in the input file. Any normal conversions will be done on numeric fields automatically, and user-provided subroutines can be invoked for specialized tasks such as text reformatting.

An important use of Transformers is the conversion of files to conform to conflicting standards and limitations imposed by various vendor software products. For example, Transformers can be generated automatically that convert structured, group-level COBOL files into contiguous-field files such as used in FORTRAN, or that reformat files containing complex COBOL data items not accessible by SAS, to simple data structures which SAS can handle.

REPORT GENERATORS NO 5

A Report Generator is based on a Data Map AND a Report Type. It is here that you specify WHICH fields (in the Data Map) are to appear WHERE (in the Report). Depending on the Report Type, you can effortlessly create background text and data output areas, or simply select desired output data by a single keystroke per field. You can specify subtotaling (up to four levels deep) and automatic or subroutine editing for any selected field.

To produce an actual report, you RUN a Report Generator. It is at this time that you specify how the report is to be sorted (up to eight sort fields, selected from the Data Map, in ascending or descending order) and what Filter—if any—is to be used for selecting records. Either on-line or batch reports can be produced from any Report Generator. Bad data is handled automatically, so you can look at incomplete or partially destroyed files. Up to eight batch reports may be generated with a single pass through a file, each using a different filter, and each sorted into a different order.

SUBFILE GENERATORS NO 6

A Subfile generator is based on a Data Map. It is used to create and generate sequential files called SUBFILES, which are extracted from parent files. A parent file can be any cataloged VSAM or physical sequential file (or any other type of file or data base for which ISO*FORM is provided an accessing subroutine). Up to eight subfiles (each specifying a different Filter and Transformer) can be generated during one pass through the parent file. Since subfiles can be extracted from other subfiles using increasingly refined filtering, ISO*FORM can be used as an infinitely flexible tool for the organized handling of a company's information base. You might, for example, want to allow a small subset of records to be repeatedly examined without the overhead of multiple passes through the major file, or to be frozen for examination as of a given date while the main file remains active (and volatile), or to be used for testing specific features of a program under development, while assuring the integrity of your live data. And since each TSO user maintains his own subfiles, there can be no conflicts.

ISO

BROCHURE
TYPOGRAPHY/DESIGN *Frank Fruzyna and Chris Satek, Chicago, Illinois* **TYPOGRAPHIC SUPPLIER** *Total Typography*
CLIENT *Isomorphic Systems* **PRINCIPAL TYPE** *Futura Condensed* **DIMENSIONS** *8½ × 11 in. (21.6 × 27.9 cm).*

ANNOUNCEMENTS
TYPOGRAPHY/DESIGN *Martin Solomon and Alexa Nosal, New York, New York* **TYPOGRAPHIC SUPPLIER** *Royal Composing Room, Inc.*
CLIENT *Royal Composing Room, Inc.* **PRINCIPAL TYPES** *Various* **DIMENSIONS** *5 × 7 in. (12.7 × 17.8 cm).*

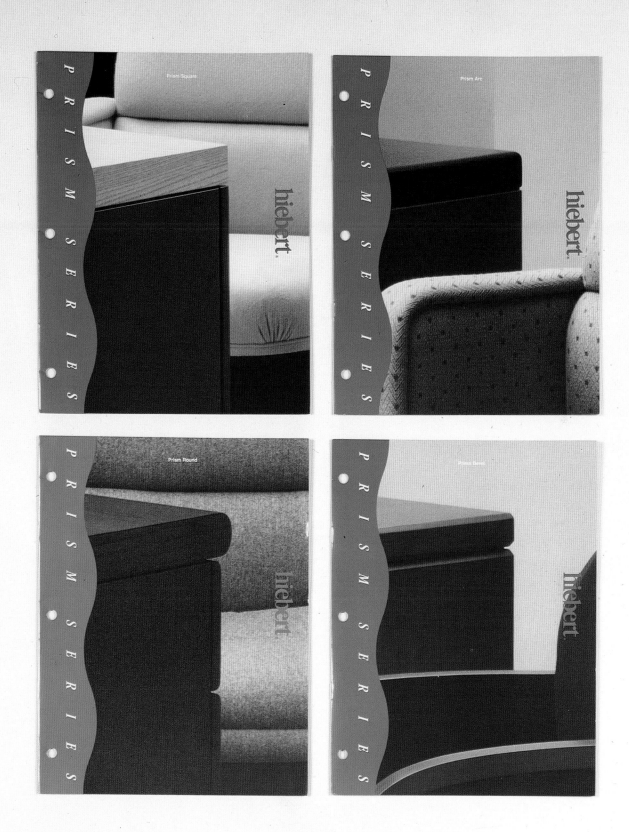

BROCHURE
TYPOGRAPHY/DESIGN *Vernon Hahn, Los Angeles, California* **ART DIRECTORS** *Jeff Fear, Ken White, and Lisa Levin Pogue*
TYPOGRAPHIC SUPPLIER *Skil-Set Typographers* **STUDIO** *White & Associates* **CLIENT** *Hiebert, Inc.* **PRINCIPAL TYPES** *ITC Garamond Book Condensed, Book Italic, and Helvetica* **DIMENSIONS** *8½ × 11 in. (21.6 × 27.9 cm).*

ANNOUNCEMENT
TYPOGRAPHY/DESIGN *D. C. Stipp, Dallas, Texas* **TYPOGRAPHIC SUPPLIER** *Southwestern Typographics* **STUDIO** *Richards Brock Miller Mitchell and Associates* **CLIENT** *Castleberry High School Class of 1976* **PRINCIPAL TYPE** *Times Roman* **DIMENSIONS** *15 × 35¼ in. (38.4 × 90.3 cm).*

POSTER
TYPOGRAPHY/DESIGN *Susan Huyser, New York, New York* **TYPOGRAPHIC SUPPLIER** *Paragon* **AGENCY** *Susan Slover Design*
CLIENT *Donghia Textiles* **PRINCIPAL TYPE** *Helvetica Condensed Bold* **DIMENSIONS** *9¼ × 37 in. (23.5 × 94 cm).*

CAMPAIGN
TYPOGRAPHY/DESIGN *Michael McPherson, Boston, Massachusetts* **TYPOGRAPHIC SUPPLIER** *Woodland Graphics* **STUDIO** *Northeastern University Publications* **CLIENT** *Art Directors Club of Boston* **PRINCIPAL TYPES** *Franklin Gothic and Century Old Style* **DIMENSIONS** *Various.*

CAMPAIGN

TYPOGRAPHY/DESIGN *Kevin Horvath, Overland Park, Kansas* **LETTERER** *Kevin Horvath* **TYPOGRAPHIC SUPPLIER** *Hallmark Cards, Inc.*
AGENCY *Hallmark Cards, Inc.* **CLIENT** *Hallmark Cards, Inc.* **PRINCIPAL TYPES** *Handlettering and ITC Avant Garde Demi Bold*
DIMENSIONS *Various.*

POSTER

TYPOGRAPHY/DESIGN *Bruce Blackburn, New York, New York* **CALLIGRAPHER** *Bruce Blackburn* **TYPOGRAPHIC SUPPLIER** *CT Typografix, Inc.*
STUDIO *Blackburn & Associates, Inc.* **CLIENT** *Napoli 99 Foundation* **PRINCIPAL TYPE** *Corbusier Stencil* **DIMENSIONS** *26⅝ × 38 in.*
(66.6 × 95 cm).

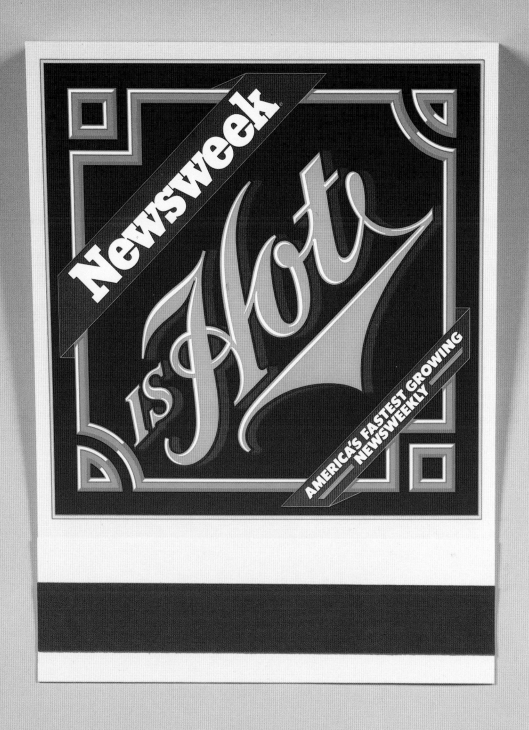

DIRECT MAIL
TYPOGRAPHY/DESIGN *Gerard Huerta and Nancy Hoefig, New York, New York* **LETTERER** *Gerard Huerta, Darien, Connecticut*
TYPOGRAPHIC SUPPLIER *Graphic Technology* **AGENCY** *Nancy Hoefig Design* **STUDIO** *Gerard Huerta Design, Inc.* **CLIENT** *Newsweek*
PRINCIPAL TYPE *Futura Extra Bold* **DIMENSIONS** *9½ × 12¾ in. (24.2 × 32.4 cm).*

LOGOTYPE
TYPOGRAPHY/DESIGN *Gerard Huerta and Phil Gips, New York, New York* **LETTERER** *Gerard Huerta, Darien, Connecticut*
AGENCY *Gips + Balkind + Associates, Inc.* **STUDIO** *Gerard Huerta Design, Inc.* **CLIENT** *The Argent Corporation.*

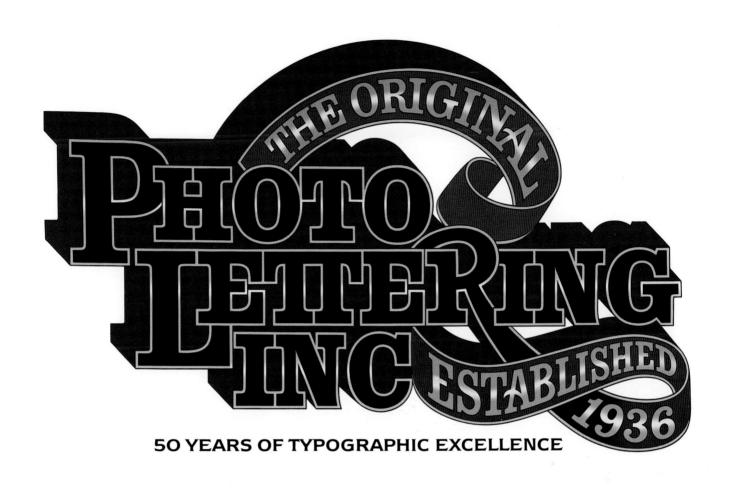

50 YEARS OF TYPOGRAPHIC EXCELLENCE

LOGOTYPE
TYPOGRAPHY/DESIGN *Ed Benguiat, New York, New York* **LETTERER** *Ed Benguiat* **TYPOGRAPHIC SUPPLIER** *Photo-Lettering, Inc.*
STUDIO *Photo-Lettering, Inc./Ed Benguiat* **CLIENT** *Photo-Lettering, Inc.* **PRINCIPAL TYPE** *Handlettering.*

PROMOTION
TYPOGRAPHY/DESIGN *James Sebastian, Michael McGinn, and François Asselin, New York, New York* **TYPOGRAPHIC SUPPLIER** *Typogram*
AGENCY *Designframe Incorporated* **CLIENT** *Champion International* **PRINCIPAL TYPE** *Univers* **DIMENSIONS** *Various.*

ADVERTISEMENT
TYPOGRAPHY/DESIGN *Luther Parson, Mary Ellen Cohen, and Michael Brennecke, New York, New York*
TYPOGRAPHIC SUPPLIER *TypoVision Plus, Inc.* **AGENCY** *Young & Rubicam New York* **CLIENT** *Time Inc., Time magazine*
PRINCIPAL TYPES *Times Roman Semi Bold and Times Roman* **DIMENSIONS** *22⅛ × 14⅞ in. (56.2 × 37.8 cm).*

BOOK
TYPOGRAPHY/DESIGN *Vance Studley, Pasadena, California* **LETTERER** *Vance Studley* **TYPOGRAPHIC SUPPLIERS** *Various*
STUDIO *Art Center College of Design* **CLIENT** *Vance Studley* **PRINCIPAL TYPES** *Various* **DIMENSIONS** *12 × 15 in. (30.5 × 38 cm).*

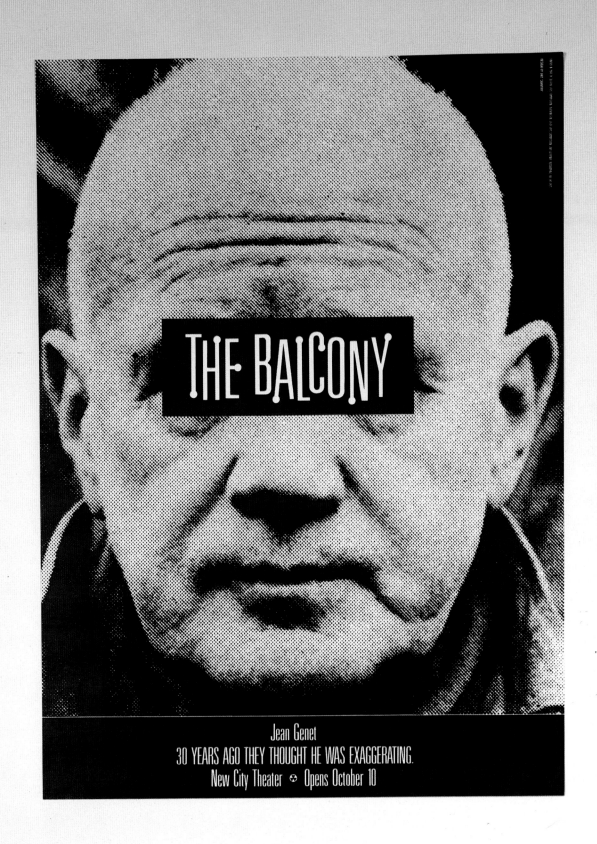

POSTER
TYPOGRAPHY/DESIGN *Art Chantry, Seattle, Washington* **LETTERER** *Art Chantry* **TYPOGRAPHIC SUPPLIER** *Eclipse Typography*
STUDIO *Art Chantry Design* **CLIENT** *The New City Theater* **PRINCIPAL TYPE** *Univers 49* **DIMENSIONS** *18 × 24 in. (46 × 61 cm).*

REGIONAL FAVORITES

Pork Tenderloin, Montgomery
*Broiled, center-cut tenderloin with onion marmalade, country sausage
and potato du jour*
$7.00

Shrimp Scampi Etouffe
A Cajun favorite served with herbed rice
$8.00

Fish of the Day
*Offering the freshest seafoods available, prepared differently each day
Market Price*

ENTREES

Breast of Chicken Dijonnaise
Sauteed breast of chicken with mustard and tarragon sauce, served with herbed rice
$7.00

Fettucine Primavera
Fettucine and garden fresh vegetables, tossed in a light cream sauce
$5.00

Filet Mignon Aux Champignons
Broiled filet mignon with smothered mushrooms served with potato du jour
$9.00

Veal Contessa
*Escalopes of veal, lightly sauteed and topped with citrus sauce
served with herbed rice*
$8.00

Poulet Au Poivre
Sauteed breast of chicken, with pepper and brandy sauce, served with herbed rice
$7.00

Peppered Cold Sliced Filet Tenderloin
With apple and horseradish sauce, served with fresh fruit
$8.00

MENU
TYPOGRAPHY/DESIGN *Jane Kelley Crowder, Houston, Texas* **CALLIGRAPHER** *Jane Kelley Crowder* **TYPOGRAPHIC SUPPLIER** *Southwest Creative Graphics* **STUDIO** *Playne Jayne Design, Inc.* **CLIENT** *Mariner Corporation for the Huntsville Marriott Hotel* **PRINCIPAL TYPE** *Palatino Italic* **DIMENSIONS** *10 × 10 in. (25.4 × 25.4 cm).*

THE NEW WILSHIRE

The hardest
working office building
in Los Angeles.

BROCHURE
TYPOGRAPHY/DESIGN *Barbara Vick, San Francisco, California* **ILLUSTRATOR** *Michael Reardon* **TYPOGRAPHIC SUPPLIER** *Reardon & Krebs*
STUDIO *Sidjakov Berman Gomez & Partners* **CLIENT** *Mahoney-Sewell/ The New Wilshire* **PRINCIPAL TYPES** *Bodoni Book and*
Franklin Gothic Condensed **DIMENSIONS** *8 × 12 in. (20.3 × 30.2 cm).*

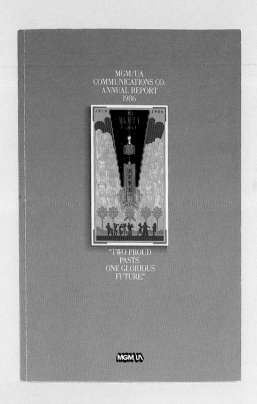

ANNUAL REPORT
TYPOGRAPHY/DESIGN *Kit Hinrichs, San Francisco, California* **TYPOGRAPHIC SUPPLIER** *Reardon & Krebs* **STUDIO** *Pentagram*
CLIENT *MGM/UA Communications Corporation* **PRINCIPAL TYPE** *Bodoni Book* **DIMENSIONS** *8 × 12 in. (20.3 × 30.5 cm).*

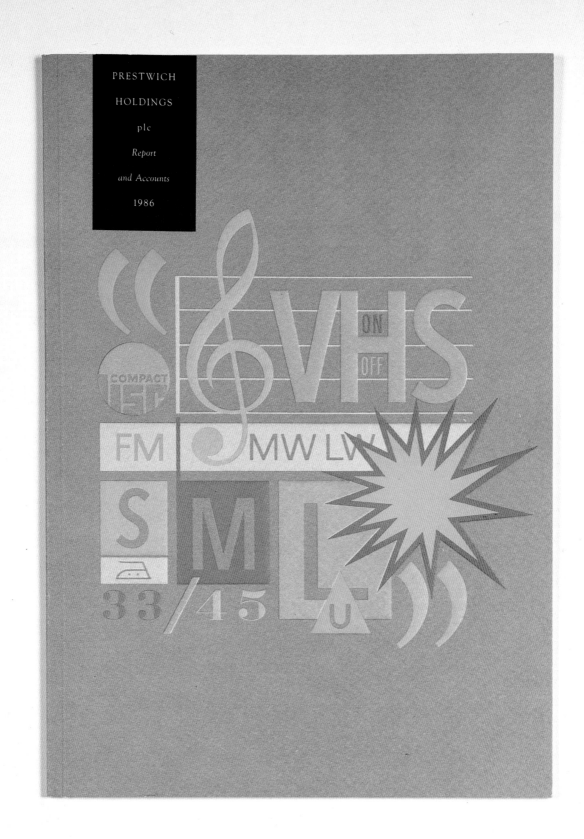

ANNUAL REPORT

TYPOGRAPHY/DESIGN *Peter Chodel, London, England* **LETTERER** *Peter Horridge, London, England* **TYPOGRAPHIC SUPPLIER** *Wordwork*
AGENCY *Michael Peters Group PLC* **STUDIO** *Michael Peters Literature Limited* **CLIENT** *Prestwich Holdings PLC* **PRINCIPAL TYPE**
Goudy Old Style **DIMENSIONS** *8¼ × 11¾ in. (21 × 29.7 cm).*

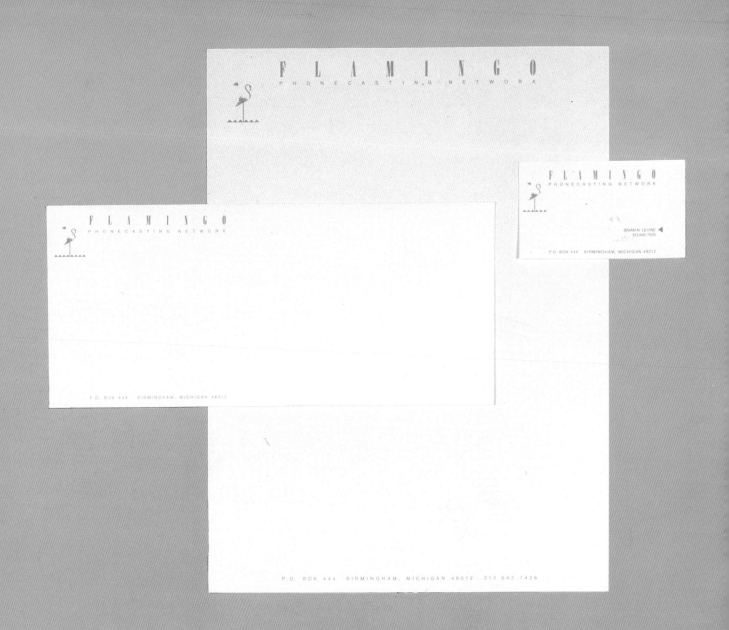

STATIONERY
TYPOGRAPHY/DESIGN *Bobbye Cochran, Chicago, Illinois* **TYPOGRAPHIC SUPPLIER** *CPS Group* **STUDIO** *Bobbye Cochran & Associates*
CLIENT *Flamingo Phonecasting Network* **PRINCIPAL TYPE** *Onyx* **DIMENSIONS** *8½ × 11 in. (21.6 × 27.9 cm).*

STATIONERY
TYPOGRAPHY/DESIGN *Lana Dyer, Albuquerque, New Mexico* **CALLIGRAPHER** *Lana Dyer* **TYPOGRAPHIC SUPPLIERS** *Copygraphics and Letraset*
STUDIO *Vaugh/Wedeen Creative, Inc.* **CLIENT** *Inn on the Alameda, Shepps New Mexico Development Corporation* **PRINCIPAL**
TYPE *Galadriel* **DIMENSIONS** *8½ × 11 in. (21.6 × 27.9 cm).*

ANNUAL REPORT
TYPOGRAPHY/DESIGN *Group 243, Inc., Carol Austin, and Janine Thielk, Ann Arbor, Michigan* **ART DIRECTOR** *Ernie Perich, Ann Arbor,*
Michigan **LETTERER** *Jerry Campbell, Southfield, Michigan* **TYPOGRAPHIC SUPPLIER** *Group 243, Inc.* **AGENCY** *Group 243, Inc.*
CLIENT *Domino's Pizza, Inc.* **PRINCIPAL TYPES** *Helvetica and Times Roman* **DIMENSIONS** *14³⁄₈ × 22³⁄₄ in. (36.5 × 57.8 cm).*

MAGAZINE
TYPOGRAPHY/DESIGN *Robert Best, New York, New York* **TYPOGRAPHIC SUPPLIER** *In-house* **CLIENT** *New York magazine*
PRINCIPAL TYPE *Century* **DIMENSIONS** *8³/₁₆ × 10⁷/₈ in. (20.8 × 27.4 cm).*

Problem-solving
at B T & R
begins with a
close look.

B T & R's professional staff knows the right questions to ask about your business needs. Our agency backgrounds give us the ability to focus on your particular talent payment or traffic problems. We can advise, or we can supplement your existing system. For example, we can conduct seminars on talent costs for your staff or help organize your traffic requirements. The result: we work more effectively for you, and you work more effectively for your clients.

Broadcast Traffic & Residuals, Inc.

BROCHURE
TYPOGRAPHY/DESIGN *Christine A. Car, New York, New York* **TYPOGRAPHIC SUPPLIER** *JCH Graphics, Ltd.*
AGENCY *Gips + Balkind + Associates/The GBA Group* **STUDIO** *Gips + Balkind + Associates/The GBA Group* **CLIENT** *Broadcast Traffic & Residuals, Inc.* **PRINCIPAL TYPE** *Lubalin Graph Bold* **DIMENSIONS** *7 × 11 in. (17.8 × 27.9 cm).*

BROCHURE
TYPOGRAPHY/DESIGN *Jennifer Morla, San Francisco, California* **TYPOGRAPHIC SUPPLIER** *Spartan Typographers*
AGENCY *Morla Design, Inc.* **STUDIO** *Morla Design, Inc. & Co.* **CLIENT** *Levi Strauss & Co.* **PRINCIPAL TYPES** *Garamond and Futura Ultra Bold* **DIMENSIONS** *11 × 14¼ in. (27.9 × 36.2 cm).*

METROPOLIS

PROMOTION IDENTITY
TYPOGRAPHY/DESIGN *Tim Girvin, Seattle, Washington* **LETTERERS** *Tim Girvin and Anton Kimball* **STUDIO** *Tim Girvin Design*
CLIENT *Nordstrom* **PRINCIPAL TYPE** *Handlettering.*

POSTER
TYPOGRAPHY/DESIGN *Gary Silverstein and John Griesel, Mountain View, California* **TYPOGRAPHIC SUPPLIER** *Frank's Type Inc.*
AGENCY *Silverstein Associates, Inc.* **CLIENT** *Silverstein Associates, Inc.* **PRINCIPAL TYPE** *Palatino Bold* **DIMENSIONS** *18 × 21⅝ in.*
(40.6 × 54.9 cm).

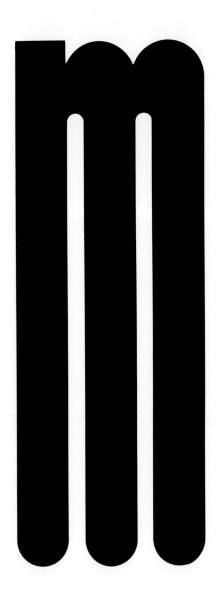

LOGOTYPE
TYPOGRAPHY/DESIGN *John Benelli, San Diego, California* **CALLIGRAPHER** *John Benelli* **STUDIO** *Benelli Design* **CLIENT** *Margie Bowles.*

STATIONERY
TYPOGRAPHY/DESIGN *John Benelli, San Diego, California* **TYPOGRAPHIC SUPPLIER** *Central Graphics* **STUDIO** *Benelli Design*
CLIENT *Margie Bowles* **PRINCIPAL TYPE** *Bodoni Book* **DIMENSIONS** *8½ × 11 in. (21.6 × 27.9 cm).*

STATIONERY
TYPOGRAPHY/DESIGN *Gina Morehead, Raleigh, North Carolina* **TYPOGRAPHIC SUPPLIER** *Phil's Photo* **AGENCY** *McKinnery &*
Silver **CLIENT** *Ric Widmer* **PRINCIPAL TYPE** *DeRoos Roman* **DIMENSIONS** *7¼ × 10½ in. (18.4 × 26.7 cm).*

IDENTITY
TYPOGRAPHY/DESIGN *Dianne Mill, Scott Sharadin, and Carl Mill, Glenside, Pennsylvania* **TYPOGRAPHIC SUPPLIER** *Typesetting etc.*
STUDIO *Art 270, Inc.* **CLIENT** *Remembrance of Things Past* **PRINCIPAL TYPE** *Carlton* **DIMENSIONS** *Various.*

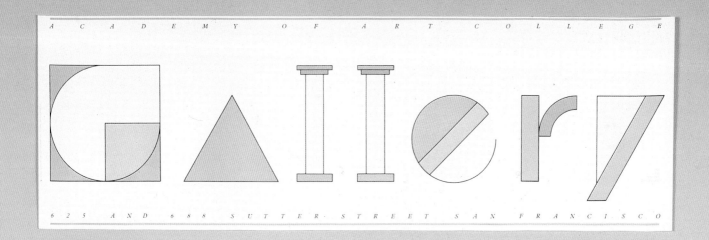

POSTER
TYPOGRAPHY/DESIGN *Sheila McCann and Michael Hall, San Francisco, California* **LETTERERS** *Sheila McCann and Michael Hall*
TYPOGRAPHIC SUPPLIER *AdCom* **AGENCY** *AdCom* **CLIENT** *Academy of Art College* **PRINCIPAL TYPE** *Handlettering*
DIMENSIONS *24½ × 7⅞ in. 62.2 × 20 cm).*

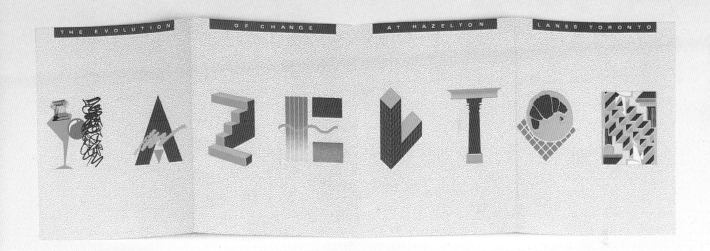

PROMOTIONAL FOLDER
TYPOGRAPHY/DESIGN *Michael Malloy, Toronto, Ontario, Canada* **LETTERER** *Taylor & Browning Design Staff, Toronto, Ontario, Canada* **TYPOGRAPHIC SUPPLIER** *Cooper & Beatty Limited* **STUDIO** *Taylor & Browning Design Associates* **CLIENT** *York Hannover Developments Limited* **PRINCIPAL TYPE** *Handlettering* **DIMENSIONS** *24 × 7½ in. (60.8 × 19.1 cm).*

BROCHURE
TYPOGRAPHY/DESIGN *Scott Eggers and Curtis Asplund, Dallas, Texas* **ILLUSTRATORS** *Curtis Asplund and Scott Eggers*
TYPOGRAPHIC SUPPLIER *Knape & Knape (in-house)* **AGENCY** *Knape & Knape* **CLIENT** *Signature Club* **PRINCIPAL TYPE** *Quorum*
DIMENSIONS *8⁹/₁₀ × 24¹/₅ (22.6 × 61.5 cm).*

GREETING CARDS

TYPOGRAPHY/DESIGN *Georgia Deaver, San Francisco, California* **CALLIGRAPHER** *Georgia Deaver* **STUDIO** *Georgia Deaver Calligraphy & Handlettering* **CLIENT** *Neugebauer Press* **DIMENSIONS** *Various.*

BROCHURE
TYPOGRAPHY/DESIGN *The Brownstone Group, Inc., Brookline, Massachusetts* **TYPOGRAPHIC SUPPLIER** *The Brownstone Group, Inc.*
STUDIO *The Brownstone Group, Inc.* **CLIENT** *The Brownstone Group, Inc.* **PRINCIPAL TYPE** *Goudy Old Style* **DIMENSIONS** *7 × 11 in.*
(17.8 × 27.9 cm).

BROCHURE
TYPOGRAPHY/DESIGN *Mario Pulice and Susan Huyser, New York, New York* **TYPOGRAPHIC SUPPLIER** *Paragon*
AGENCY *Susan Slover Design* **CLIENT** *Winthrop Hill* **PRINCIPAL TYPE** *Trade Gothic* **DIMENSIONS** *5 × 11 in. (12.7 × 27.9 cm).*

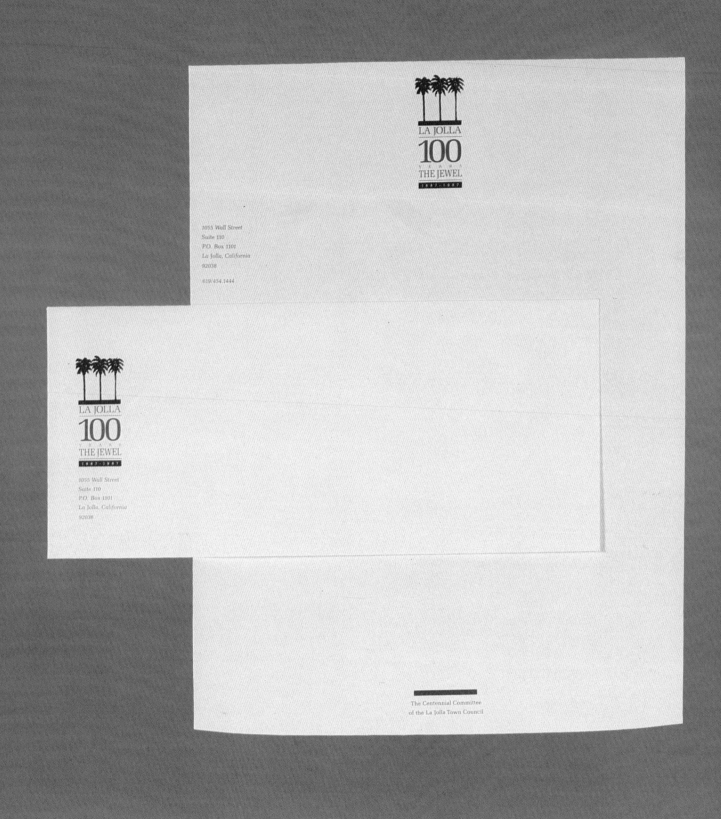

STATIONERY
TYPOGRAPHY/DESIGN *David Alcorn, La Jolla, California* **TYPOGRAPHIC SUPPLIERS** *Central Graphics and Advance Graphics*
AGENCY *Alcorn Visual Communications* **CLIENT** *La Jolla Town Council* **PRINCIPAL TYPE** *Melior* **DIMENSIONS** *8½ × 11 in.*
(21.6 × 27.9 cm).

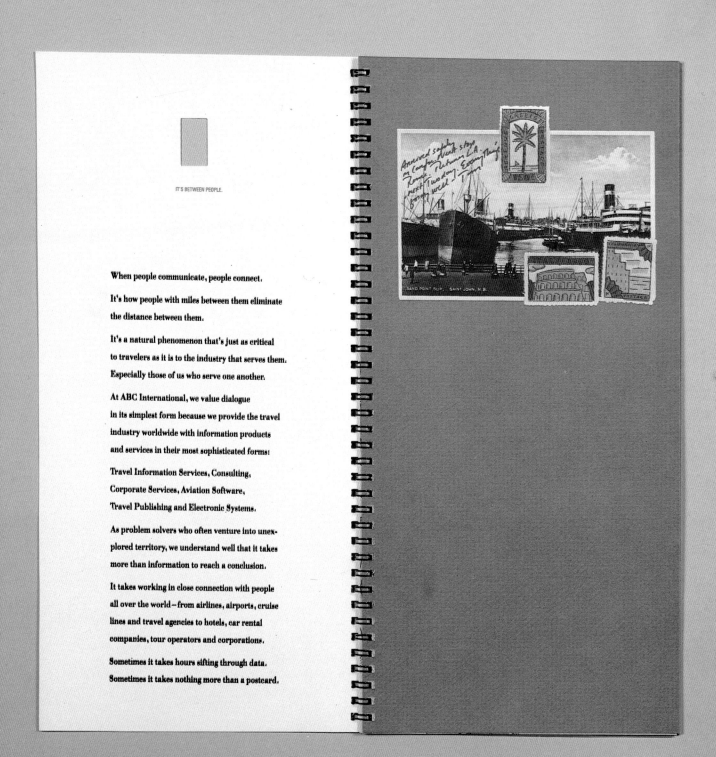

IT'S BETWEEN PEOPLE.

When people communicate, people connect.

It's how people with miles between them eliminate
the distance between them.

It's a natural phenomenon that's just as critical
to travelers as it is to the industry that serves them.
Especially those of us who serve one another.

At ABC International, we value dialogue
in its simplest form because we provide the travel
industry worldwide with information products
and services in their most sophisticated forms:

Travel Information Services, Consulting,
Corporate Services, Aviation Software,
Travel Publishing and Electronic Systems.

As problem solvers who often venture into unex-
plored territory, we understand well that it takes
more than information to reach a conclusion.

It takes working in close connection with people
all over the world—from airlines, airports, cruise
lines and travel agencies to hotels, car rental
companies, tour operators and corporations.

Sometimes it takes hours sifting through data.
Sometimes it takes nothing more than a postcard.

BROCHURE
TYPOGRAPHY/DESIGN *Holly Russell, Boston Massachusetts* **TYPOGRAPHIC SUPPLIER** *Typographic House* **AGENCY** *Altman & Manley, Inc.*
STUDIO *Altman & Manley, Inc./Design* **CLIENT** *ABC International, Inc.* **PRINCIPAL TYPE** *Bodoni* **DIMENSIONS** *7 × 14 in.*
(17.3 × 35.3 cm).

The British Letter Foundry

A new type on improved principles, cut by Richard
Austin for John Bell. The quality of the engraving

SANS SERIF was introduced in the 1820s
as a display type, but it was a hundred years
before it was modified to a suitable text type

Justus Erich Walbaum, founder

at Weimar, cut this type around 1803. His capitals
are wider than Bodoni's, the curved elements more
rectangular. He mitigated the mechanical rigidity
of the typeface's modern stress to a certain degree

THE STANDARD European type of the sixteenth
& seventeenth centuries was the Garamond roman,
an old style type based on Aldus' types and probably
cut by Claude Garamont for Robert Estienne in Paris
in 1531. Around 1550 taller capitals were cut. Follow-

About 1722 William Caslon

cut the type which bears his name after
the sensible if homely style of Van Dijck. While the Con-
tinental founders had adopted the lighter model of copper
engraving, Caslon preferred the 'broken-in' look of the preceding
century. Some characters are quite peculiar, but the massed effect is
vigorous & legible, making it suitable for all manner of bookwork.

WILLIAM BULMER raised the Art of Fine Printing
in England—though it had not been particularly high
prior to the Efforts of BASKERVILLE. Bulmer's types
WILLIAM MARTIN, brother of BASKER-
and engraving is by BEWICK.

The Development of

BOOK TYPES

Illustrated in Compositions from the Cases
at POLTROON PRESS

First Series
Revised and Expanded

BERKELEY
1986

POSTCARD SET
TYPOGRAPHY/DESIGN *Alastair Johnston, Berkeley, California* **TYPOGRAPHIC SUPPLIER** *Poltroon Press* **STUDIO** *Poltroon Press &
Novelty Company* **CLIENT** *Poltroon Press & Novelty Company* **PRINCIPAL TYPES** *Foundry Hall and Foundry Futura*
DIMENSIONS *4 × 6 in. (10.2 × 15.2 cm).*

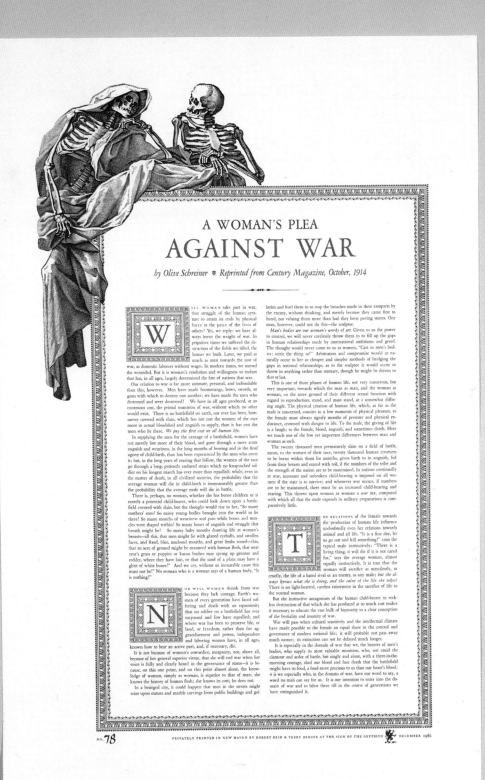

BROADSIDE
TYPOGRAPHY/DESIGN *Robert R. Reid, New Haven, Connecticut* **TYPOGRAPHIC SUPPLIER** *The private press of Robert Reid and Terry Berger*
STUDIO *The Sign of the Gryphon* **CLIENT** *Robert Reid and Terry Berger* **PRINCIPAL TYPES** *Linotype Granjon and ATF Garamond*
DIMENSIONS *16⅝ × 25 in. (42.2 × 63.5 cm).*

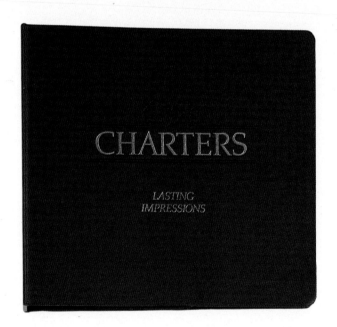

BOOK
TYPOGRAPHY/DESIGN *Jon Vopni and Robert Hyland, Toronto, Ontario, Canada* **CALLIGRAPHERS** *Larry Bloss and Frank Bonigut*
LETTERERS *Alf Ebson, George Kay, and Jon Vopni* **TYPOGRAPHIC SUPPLIER** *Type Studio, Cooper & Beatty Limited* **STUDIO** *Robert Hyland Design* **CLIENT** *M.C. Charters & Company Limited* **PRINCIPAL TYPE** *Palatino Italic* **DIMENSIONS** *8½ × 9½ in. (21.6 × 24.1 cm).*

BROCHURE
TYPOGRAPHY/DESIGN *Vicki Navratil, New York, New York* **WRITER** *Evan Juro and Associates, Inc.* **TYPOGRAPHIC SUPPLIER** *MJ Baumwell* **AGENCY** *Cosgrove Juro* **CLIENT** *Citicorp Investor Relations* **PRINCIPAL TYPE** *Administer Light* **DIMENSIONS** *8½ × 11 in. (21.6 × 27.9 cm).*

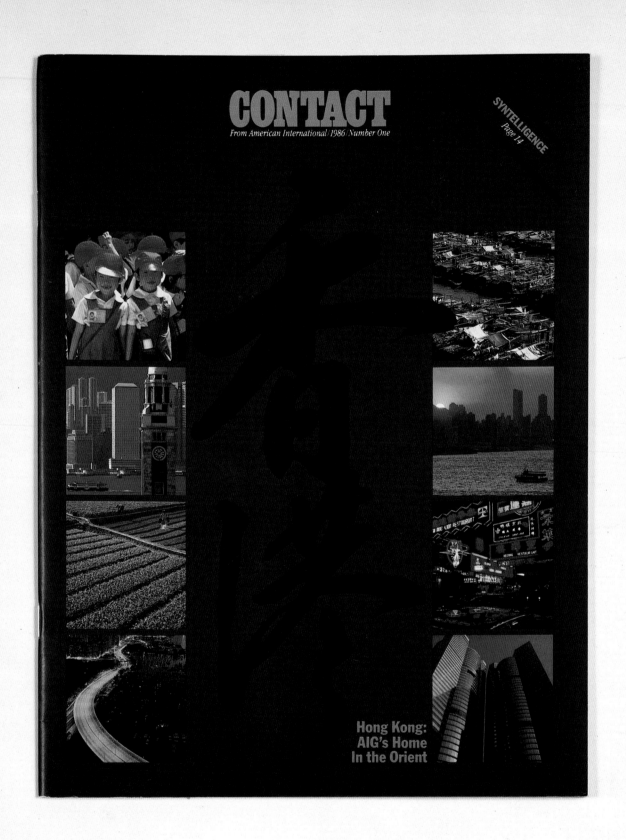

MAGAZINE
TYPOGRAPHY/DESIGN *David Barnett and Dennis Barnett, New York, New York* **TYPOGRAPHIC SUPPLIER** *Expertype, Inc.*
STUDIO *Barnett Design Group, Inc.* **CLIENT** *American International Group* **PRINCIPAL TYPES** *Garamond and Franklin Gothic*
DIMENSIONS *8½ × 11 in. (21.6 × 27.9 cm).*

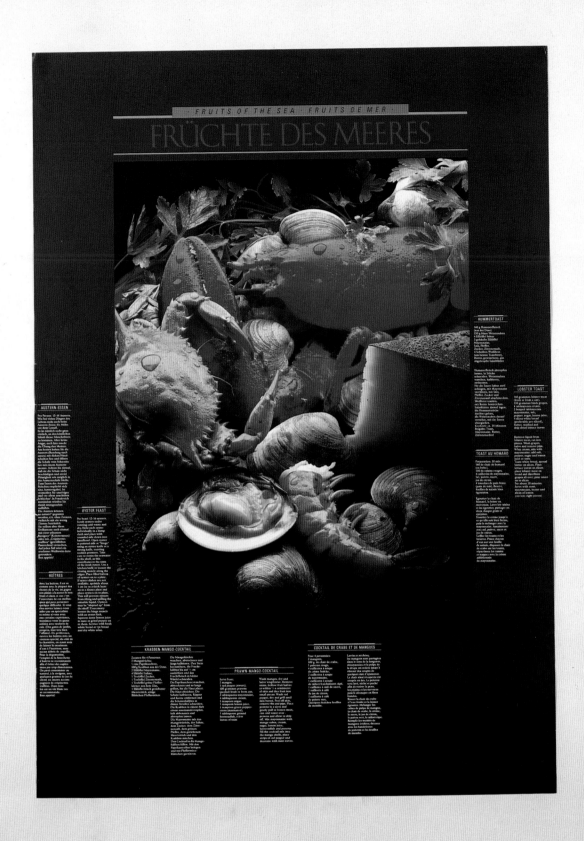

POSTER

TYPOGRAPHY/DESIGN *Olaf Leu and Fritz Hofrichter, Frankfurt, West Germany* **TYPOGRAPHIC SUPPLIER** *Con Composition GmbH*
STUDIO *Olaf Leu Design & Partner* **CLIENT** *Druckfarbenfabrik Gebr. Schmidt GmbH* **PRINCIPAL TYPES** *Schneidler Initialen,*
Schneidler Halbfett, and Univers 57 **DIMENSIONS** *27½ × 37⅜ in. (70 × 95 cm).*

STATIONERY
TYPOGRAPHY/DESIGN *Diana Graham and Joyce Ho, New York, New York* **TYPOGRAPHIC SUPPLIER** *JCH Graphics*
STUDIO *Diagram Design and Marketing Communications, Inc.* **PRINCIPAL TYPE** *Bodoni Book* **DIMENSIONS** *8½ × 11 in. (21.6 × 28 cm).*

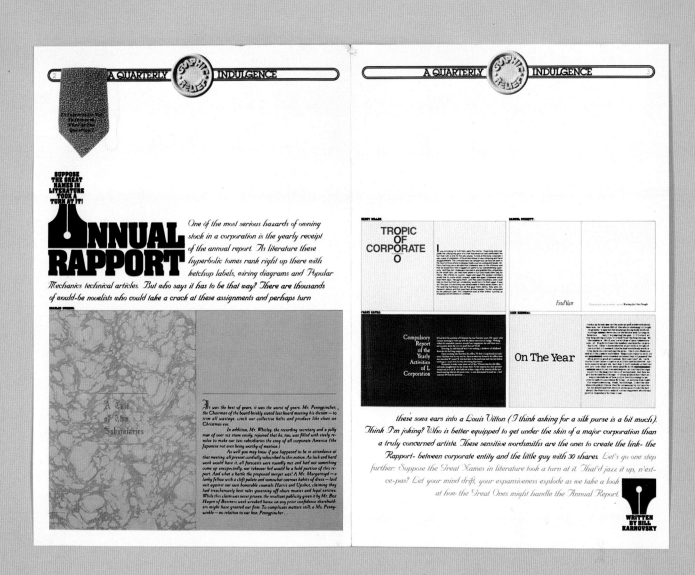

EDITORIAL

TYPOGRAPHY/DESIGN *David Brier, East Rutherford, New Jersey* **LETTERER** *David Brier* **TYPOGRAPHIC SUPPLIER** *Pulsar Graphics Inc.* **STUDIO** *David Brier Design Works, Inc.* **CLIENT** *Graphic Relief/David Brier Design Works, Inc.* **PRINCIPAL TYPES** *Aachen Bold and Nuptial* **DIMENSIONS** *17½ × 23 in. (22.5 × 58.4 cm).*

Woodward's Annual Report
for the fiscal year ended
January 25, 1986.
It was a year unlike any
other in the history of Woodward's.
The Company updated its
merchandising strategy to meet the
challenges of today's
marketplace. We continued
our major renovation
program to add flair and
excitement to ...

ANNUAL REPORT
TYPOGRAPHY/DESIGN *John Van Dyke, Seattle, Washington* **TYPOGRAPHIC SUPPLIER** *Pola Graphics* **AGENCY** *Van Dyke Company*
CLIENT *Woodward's Stores, Ltd.* **PRINCIPAL TYPES** *Garamond No. 3, Didi, and Helvetica Heavy* **DIMENSIONS** *9 × 12 in.*
(22.9 × 30.5 cm).

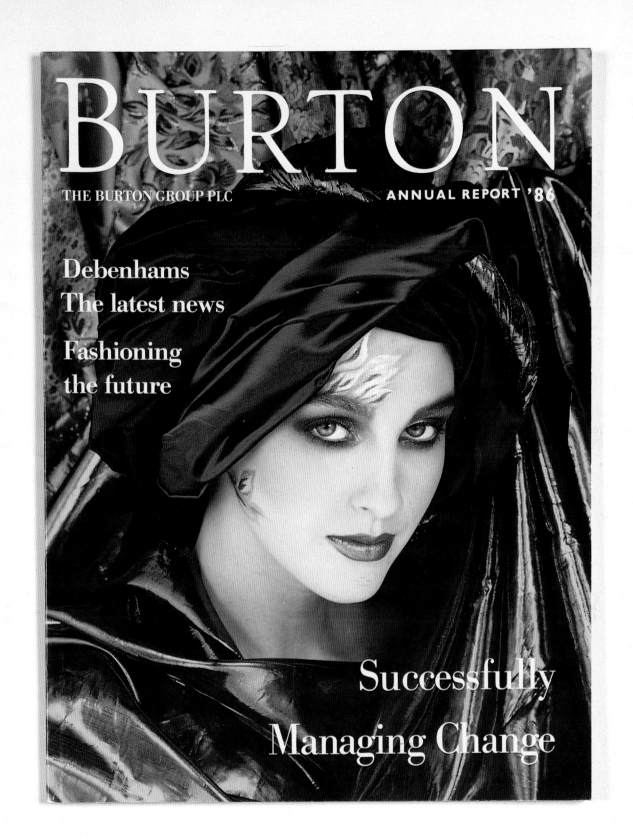

BURTON

THE BURTON GROUP PLC   ANNUAL REPORT '86

Debenhams
The latest news

Fashioning
the future

Successfully

Managing Change

ANNUAL REPORT
TYPOGRAPHY/DESIGN *David Stocks and Nick Austin, London, England* **ART DIRECTOR** *Michael Peters, London, England*
LETTERERS *David Stocks and Nick Austin* **TYPOGRAPHIC SUPPLIER** *Acesetters* **AGENCY** *Michael Peters Group PLC*
STUDIO *Michael Peters Literature Limited* **CLIENT** *Burton Group PLC* **PRINCIPAL TYPE** *Bodoni Antiqua*
DIMENSIONS *9 × 11⁷⁄₈ in. (23 × 30 cm).*

Thoughts to Ponder: LESSONS FROM GEESE

Next time you see geese heading south for the winter, flying along in V formation, you might be interested in knowing what science has discovered about why they fly that way. It has been learned that as each bird flaps its wings, it creates an uplift for the bird immediately following. By flying in a V formation, the whole flock adds at least 71 percent greater flying range than if each bird flew on its own. Whenever a goose falls out of formation, it suddenly feels the drag and resistance of trying to go it alone and quickly gets back into formation to take advantage of the lifting power of the bird in front. When the lead goose gets tired, he rotates back in the wing and another goose flies point. The geese honk from behind to encourage those up front to keep up their speed. Finally, when a goose gets sick, or is wounded by gunshot and falls out, two geese fall out of formation and follow him down to help and protect him. They stay with him until he is able to fly, or until he is dead; and then launch out on their own or with another formation to catch up with their original group. You see, all we have to do in order to attract those who are not participating is to demonstrate to the world that we have as much sense as a goose. That seems like enough price to pay to win the lost and to help one another.

Adapted from Barbara Sterling Willson

The 1986 United Way Campaign

CERTIFICATE
TYPOGRAPHY/DESIGN *Josanne Nowak, Rochester, New York* **CALLIGRAPHER** *Josanne Nowak* **TYPOGRAPHIC SUPPLIER** *Total Typography* **STUDIO** *Lichtenstein Marketing Communications* **CLIENT** *Xerox Corporation United Way Campaign* **PRINCIPAL TYPES** *ITC Garamond Book Italic and handlettering* **DIMENSIONS** *11 × 14 in. (35.5 × 28.2 cm).*

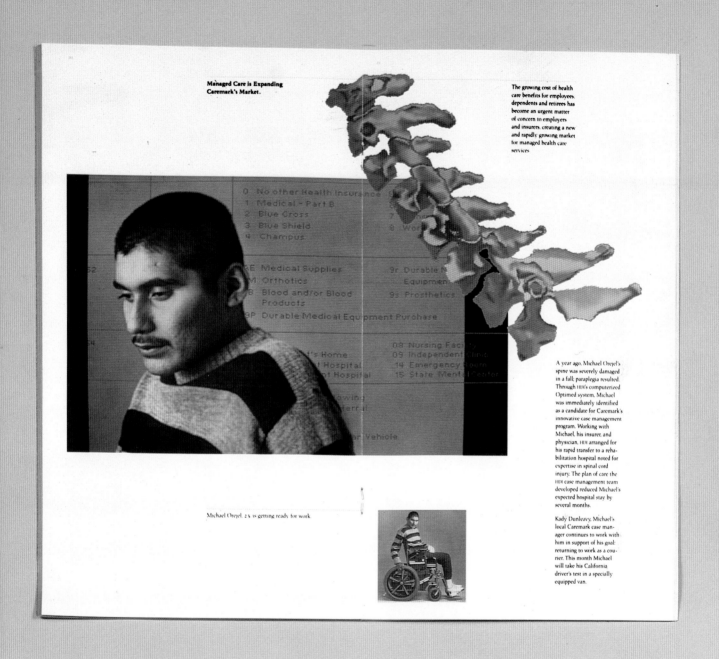

Managed Care is Expanding Caremark's Market.

The growing cost of health care benefits for employees, dependents and retirees has become an urgent matter of concern to employers and insurers, creating a new and rapidly growing market for managed health care services.

0. No other Health Insurance
1. Medical - Part B
2. Blue Cross
3. Blue Shield
4. Champus

E Medical Supplies
M Orthotics
B Blood and/or Blood Products
9P Durable Medical Equipment Purchase

9r Durable N Equipment
9s Prosthetics

09 Nursing Facility
09 Independent Clinic
14 Emergency Room
15 State Mental Center

Michael Orejel, 23, is getting ready for work.

A year ago, Michael Orejel's spine was severely damaged in a fall; paraplegia resulted. Through HDI's computerized Optimed system, Michael was immediately identified as a candidate for Caremark's innovative case management program. Working with Michael, his insurer, and physician, HDI arranged for his rapid transfer to a rehabilitation hospital noted for expertise in spinal cord injury. The plan of care the HDI case management team developed reduced Michael's expected hospital stay by several months.

Kady Dunleavy, Michael's local Caremark case manager continues to work with him in support of his goal: returning to work as a courier. This month Michael will take his California driver's test in a specially equipped van.

ANNUAL REPORT
TYPOGRAPHY/DESIGN *Jim Berte and Robert Miles Runyan & Associates, Playa del Rey, California* **STUDIO** *Robert Miles Runyan & Associates* **CLIENT** *Caremark, Inc.* **PRINCIPAL TYPE** *Aldus* **DIMENSIONS** *12 × 7 in. (30.5 × 17.8 cm).*

INVITATION

TYPOGRAPHY/DESIGN *Stephen P. Miller, Dallas, Texas* **TYPOGRAPHIC SUPPLIER** *Southwestern Typographics* **STUDIO** *Richards Brock Miller Mitchell and Associates* **CLIENT** *Vecta Contract* **PRINCIPAL TYPE** *Franklin Gothic* **DIMENSIONS** $27^3/_4 \times 11^1/_2$ *in.* *(70.5 × 29.2 cm).*

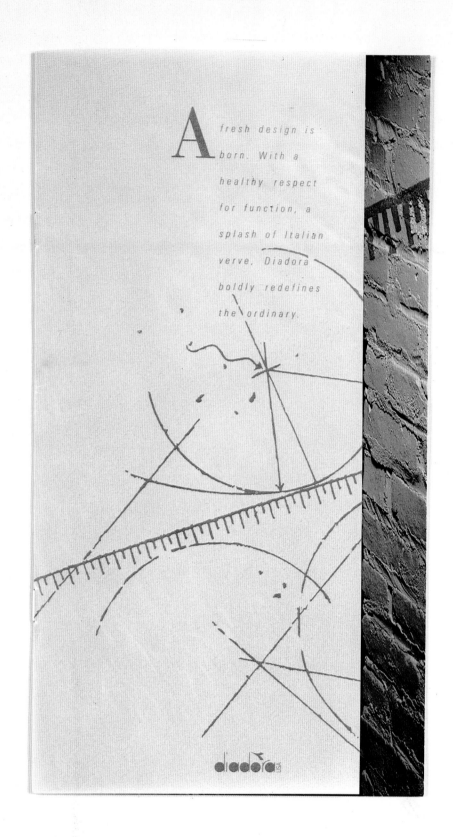

A fresh design is born. With a healthy respect for function, a splash of Italian verve, Diadora boldly redefines the ordinary.

CATALOG
TYPOGRAPHY/DESIGN *Jack Anderson and Cheri Huber, Seattle, Washington* **TYPOGRAPHIC SUPPLIER** *The Type Gallery*
STUDIO *Hornall Anderson Design Works* **CLIENT** *Mac B Sports* **PRINCIPAL TYPES** *Univers 48 Italic and Bodoni Book*
DIMENSIONS *6 × 11 in. (15.2 × 27.9 cm).*

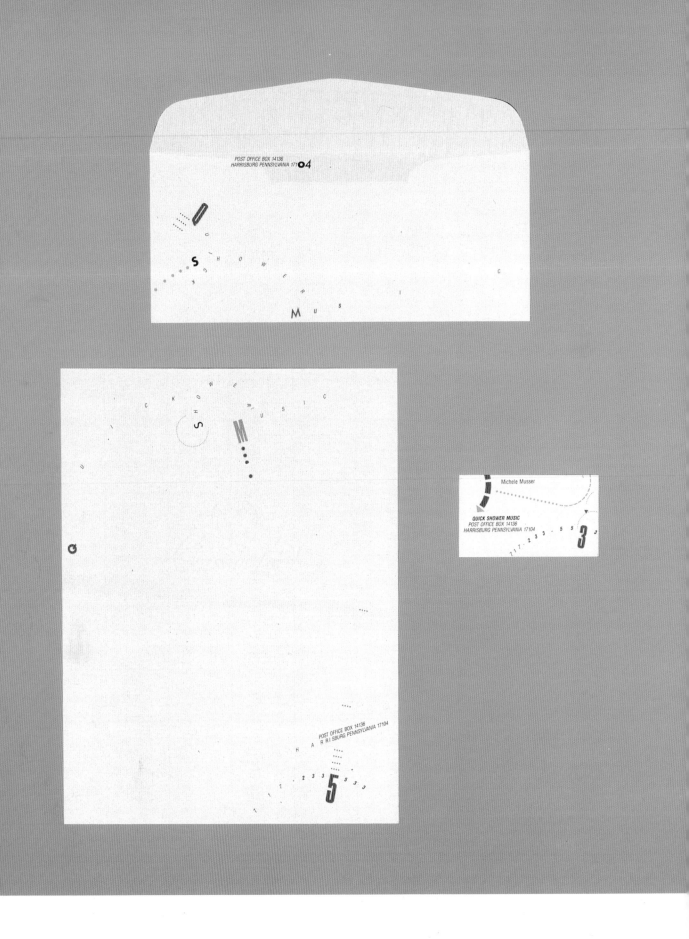

STATIONERY

TYPOGRAPHY/DESIGN *Jerry King Musser, Harrisburg, Pennsylvania* **TYPOGRAPHIC SUPPLIER** *Reprographics Typography* **STUDIO** *Musser Design* **CLIENT** *Quick Shower Music* **PRINCIPAL TYPE** *Helvetica* **DIMENSIONS** *8½ × 11 in. (21.6 × 27.9 cm).*

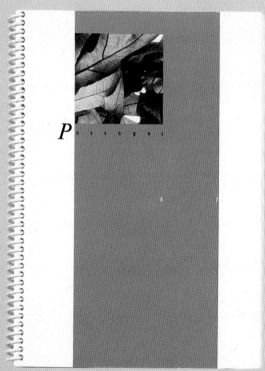

CALENDAR
TYPOGRAPHY/DESIGN *Craig Minor and Cheryl Brzezinski, Houston, Texas* **TYPOGRAPHIC SUPPLIER** *Characters* **STUDIO** *Creel Morrell Inc.*
CLIENT *Creel Morrell, Inc.* **PRINCIPAL TYPES** *Futura Bold Condensed and Times Roman* **DIMENSIONS** *6 × 8½ in. (15.2 × 21.6 cm).*

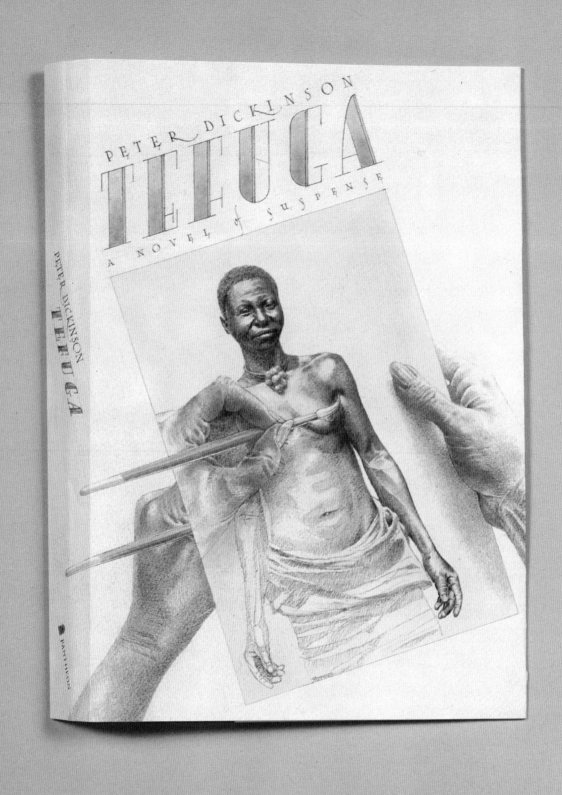

BOOK JACKET
TYPOGRAPHY/DESIGN *Dugald Stermer, San Francisco, California* **LETTERER** *Dugald Stermer* **CLIENT** *Pantheon Books*
PRINCIPAL TYPE *Handlettering* **DIMENSIONS** *5⁹/₁₆ × 8⁷/₁₆ in. (14.1 × 21.4 cm).*

BOOK
TYPOGRAPHY/DESIGN *Susan Mitchell, Stamford, Connecticut* **TYPOGRAPHIC SUPPLIER** *Maryland Linotype Composition Company*
CLIENT *Pantheon Books* **PRINCIPAL TYPE** *Linotype Waverly* **DIMENSIONS** *4½ × 7¼ in. (11.4 × 18.4 cm).*

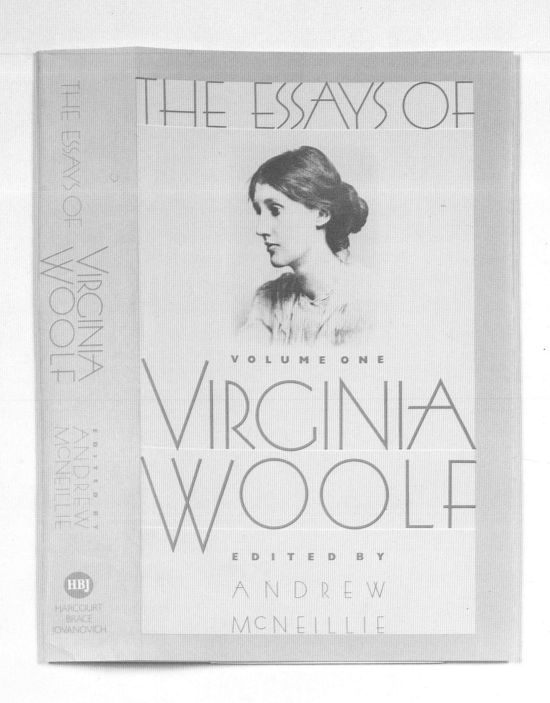

BOOK JACKET
TYPOGRAPHY/DESIGN *Louise Fili, New York, New York* **CALLIGRAPHER** *Louise Fili* **CLIENT** *Harcourt Brace Jovanovich*
PRINCIPAL TYPE *Handlettering* **DIMENSIONS** *6⅛ × 9¼ in. (17.3 × 23.5 cm).*

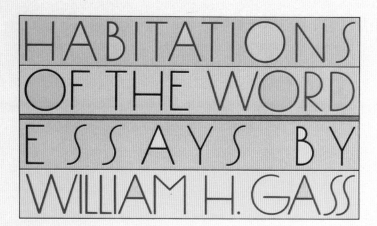

"Words are with us everywhere. In our erotic secrecies, in our sleep. We're often no more aware of them than our own spit, although we use them oftener than legs. So of course in the customary shallow unconscious sense, we comprehend the curse, the prayer, and the whoop."

BOOK
TYPOGRAPHY/DESIGN *Paula Scher, New York, New York* **TYPOGRAPHIC SUPPLIER** *Personal collection of Paula Scher*
STUDIO *Koppel & Scher* **CLIENT** *Simon & Schuster* **PRINCIPAL TYPE** *Harpers* **DIMENSIONS** *6½ × 9¼ in. (16.5 × 23.5 cm).*

BOOK JACKET
TYPOGRAPHY/DESIGN *Lorraine Louie, New York, New York* **LETTERER** *Daniel Pelavin, New York, New York*
STUDIO *Lorraine Louie Design* **CLIENT** *Alfred A. Knopf* **PRINCIPAL TYPE** *Handlettering* **DIMENSIONS** *6⁵/₁₆ × 9⁷/₁₆ in. (16 × 24 cm).*

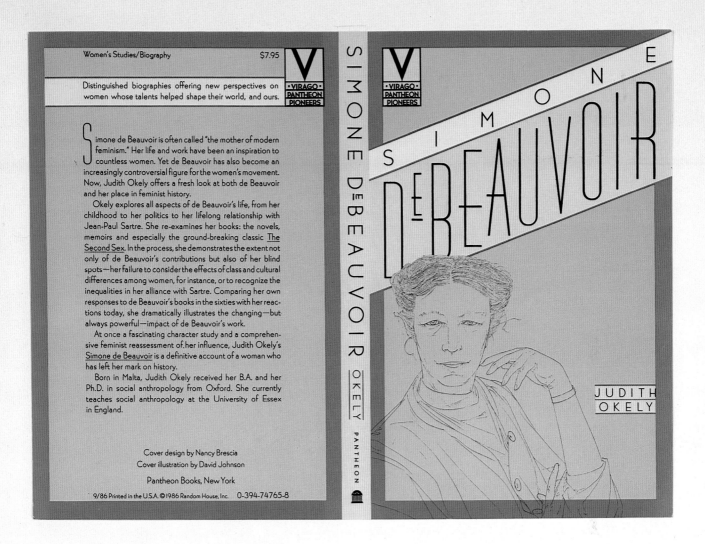

Women's Studies/Biography $7.95

Distinguished biographies offering new perspectives on
women whose talents helped shape their world, and ours.

Simone de Beauvoir is often called "the mother of modern
feminism." Her life and work have been an inspiration to
countless women. Yet de Beauvoir has also become an
increasingly controversial figure for the women's movement.
Now, Judith Okely offers a fresh look at both de Beauvoir
and her place in feminist history.

Okely explores all aspects of de Beauvoir's life, from her
childhood to her politics to her lifelong relationship with
Jean-Paul Sartre. She re-examines her books: the novels,
memoirs and especially the ground-breaking classic The
Second Sex. In the process, she demonstrates the extent not
only of de Beauvoir's contributions but also of her blind
spots—her failure to consider the effects of class and cultural
differences among women, for instance, or to recognize the
inequalities in her alliance with Sartre. Comparing her own
responses to de Beauvoir's books in the sixties with her reac-
tions today, she dramatically illustrates the changing—but
always powerful—impact of de Beauvoir's work.

At once a fascinating character study and a comprehen-
sive feminist reassessment of her influence, Judith Okely's
Simone de Beauvoir is a definitive account of a woman who
has left her mark on history.

Born in Malta, Judith Okely received her B.A. and her
Ph.D. in social anthropology from Oxford. She currently
teaches social anthropology at the University of Essex
in England.

Cover design by Nancy Brescia
Cover illustration by David Johnson

Pantheon Books, New York

9/86 Printed in the U.S.A. © 1986 Random House, Inc.   0-394-74765-8

SIMONE DeBEAUVOIR OKELY   PANTHEON

SIMONE DeBEAUVOIR

JUDITH OKELY

BOOK COVER
TYPOGRAPHY/DESIGN *Nancy Brescia, New York, New York* **TYPOGRAPHIC SUPPLIER** *The Type Shop* **CLIENT** *Pantheon Books*
PRINCIPAL TYPES *Huxley Vertical and Bernhard Gothic Light* **DIMENSIONS** *5½ × 8¼ in. (14 × 21 cm).*

POSTER
TYPOGRAPHY/DESIGN *Dianne Mill, Glenside, Pennsylvania* **TYPOGRAPHIC SUPPLIER** *Typesetting etc.* **STUDIO** *Art 270, Inc.*
CLIENT *Tyler School of Art* **PRINCIPAL TYPES** *ITC Tiffany Demi and ITC Garamond Medium* **DIMENSIONS** *22 × 31³⁄₄ in.*
(55.9 × 80.6 cm).

STATIONERY
TYPOGRAPHY/DESIGN *Julie Frankel, Cela Wright, and Rebecca Bourbeau, Boston, Massachusetts* **TYPOGRAPHIC SUPPLIER** *Monotype*
STUDIO *Frankel & Wright Associates, Inc.* **CLIENT** *Frankel & Wright Associates, Inc.* **PRINCIPAL TYPES** *ITC Garamond Bold
Condensed, Times Roman, and Zapf Bold* **DIMENSIONS** *8¹/₂ × 11 in. (21.6 × 27.9 cm).*

BROCHURE
TYPOGRAPHY/DESIGN *Jim Hackley, Baltimore, Maryland* **TYPOGRAPHIC SUPPLIER** *Brushwood Graphics* **STUDIO** *North Charles Street Design Organization* **CLIENT** *Grace and Saint Peter's School* **PRINCIPAL TYPES** *Goudy Old Style and Franklin Gothic* **DIMENSIONS** *8½ × 5½ in. (21.6 × 14 cm).*

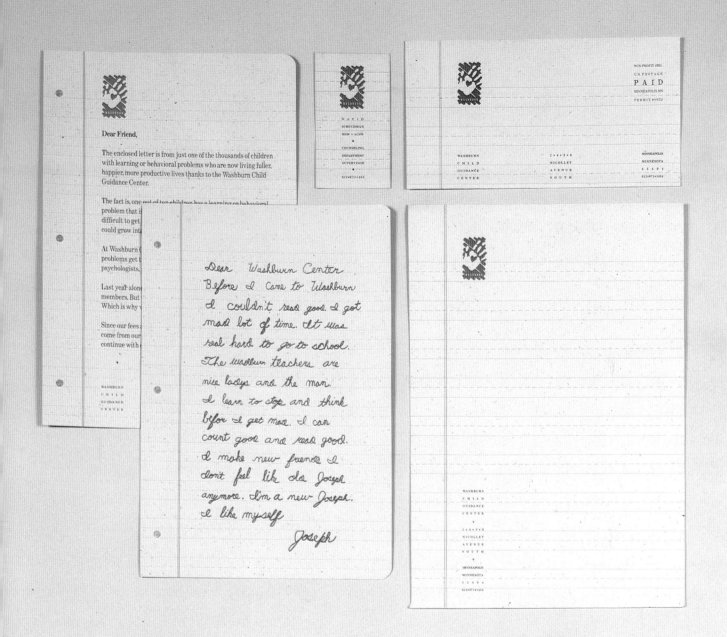

BOOK
TYPOGRAPHY/DESIGN *Charles Spencer Anderson, Minneapolis, Minnesota* **TYPOGRAPHIC SUPPLIER** *Typeshooters*
STUDIO *Duffy Design Group* **CLIENT** *Washburn Child Guidance Center* **PRINCIPAL TYPES** *Century Schoolbook and Century Schoolbook Italic*
DIMENSIONS *6½ × 9¼ in. (16.5 × 23.5 cm).*

CATALOG
TYPOGRAPHY/DESIGN *Neil Shakery, San Francisco, California* **TYPOGRAPHIC SUPPLIER** *Walker Graphics* **STUDIO** *Pentagram*
CLIENT *Banana Republic* **PRINCIPAL TYPE** *ITC Century Light Condensed* **DIMENSIONS** *5⅜ × 8⅜ in. (13.6 × 21.3 cm).*

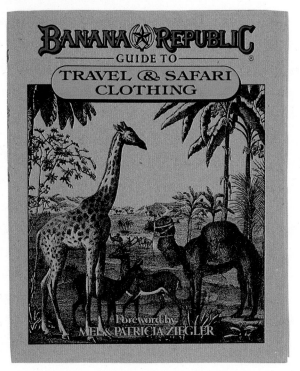

BOOK

TYPOGRAPHY/DESIGN *Alex Jay, Studio J (text) and Jimmy Harris (jacket), New York, New York* **TYPOGRAPHIC SUPPLIER** *TGA Communications* **CLIENT** *Ballantine Books* **PRINCIPAL TYPES** *ITC Cushing (text), and ITC Barcelona and Mel Ziegler's Typewriter (display)* **DIMENSIONS** *8 × 10 in. (20.3 × 25.4 cm).*

ANNOUNCEMENT
TYPOGRAPHY/DESIGN *Charles Spencer Anderson and Sharon Werner, Minneapolis, Minnesota* **TYPOGRAPHIC SUPPLIER** *Typeshooters*
STUDIO *Duffy Design Group* **CLIENT** *Nancy Bundt Photography* **PRINCIPAL TYPE** *Helvetica Condensed* **DIMENSIONS** *35³⁄₈ × 12 in.*
(89.5 × 30.5 cm).

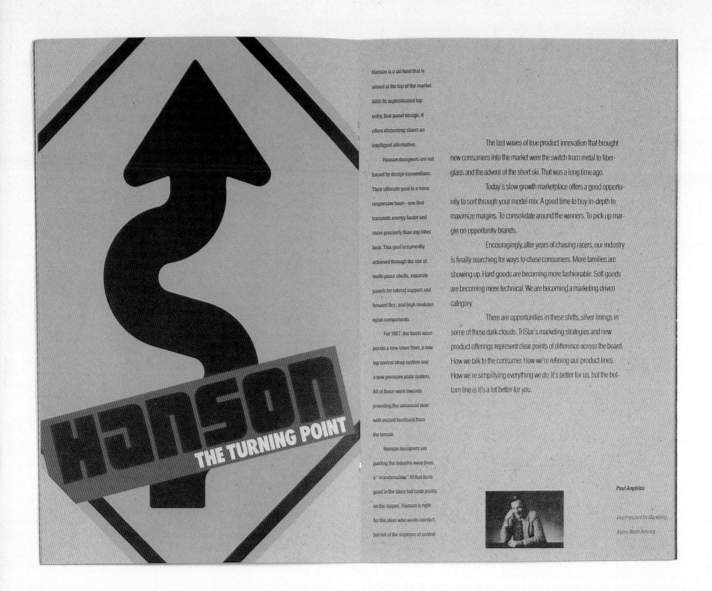

BROCHURE
TYPOGRAPHY/DESIGN *Paul Huber, Boston, Massachusetts* **TYPOGRAPHIC SUPPLIER** *Typographic House* **AGENCY** *Altman & Manley,*
Inc. **STUDIO** *Altman & Manley, Inc./Design* **CLIENT** *TriStar Sports, Inc.* **PRINCIPAL TYPES** *Helvetica Light and Helvetica Bold*
Condensed **DIMENSIONS** *9 × 14 in. (23 × 35.5 cm).*

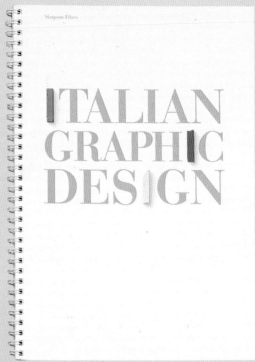

BOOK
TYPOGRAPHY/DESIGN *Michael Mescal and James Cross, Los Angeles, California* **TYPOGRAPHIC SUPPLIER** *Andresen Typographers*
STUDIO *Cross Associates* **CLIENT** *Simpson Paper Company* **PRINCIPAL TYPE** *Bodoni* **DIMENSIONS** *11½ × 8 in. (20.3 × 29.2 cm).*

BOOK COVER
TYPOGRAPHY/DESIGN *Carin Goldberg, New York, New York* **TYPOGRAPHIC SUPPLIER** *The Type Shop* **STUDIO** *Carin Goldberg Design*
CLIENT *Vintage Books* **PRINCIPAL TYPE** *Futura Bold Condensed* **DIMENSIONS** *6⅛ × 9¼ in. (15.5 × 23.5 cm).*

179

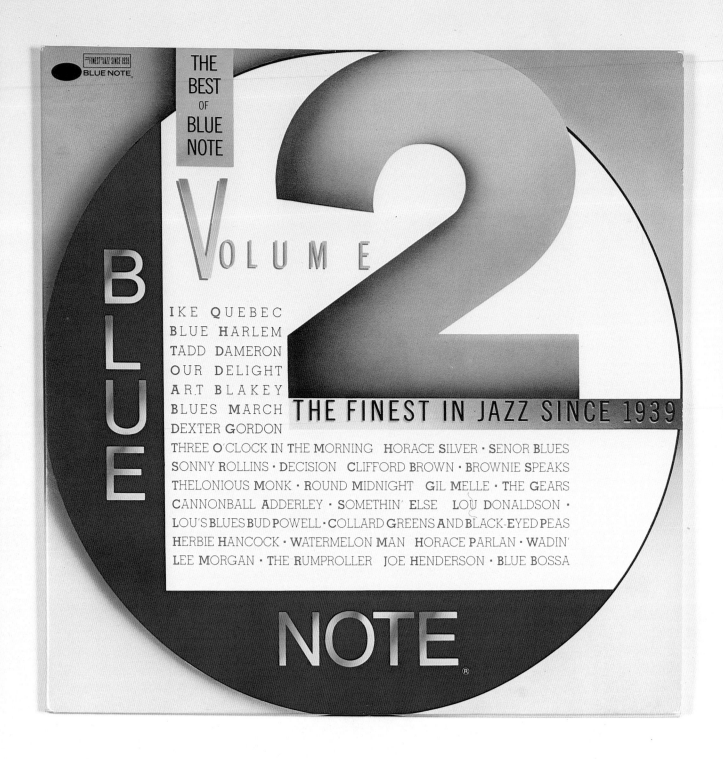

RECORD ALBUM COVER
TYPOGRAPHY/DESIGN *Paula Scher, New York, New York* **TYPOGRAPHIC SUPPLIER** *The Type Shop* **STUDIO** *Koppel & Scher*
CLIENT *Manhattan Records* **PRINCIPAL TYPES** *Alternate Gothic and Stymie* **DIMENSIONS** *12³/₈ × 12³/₈ in. (31.4 × 31.4 cm).*

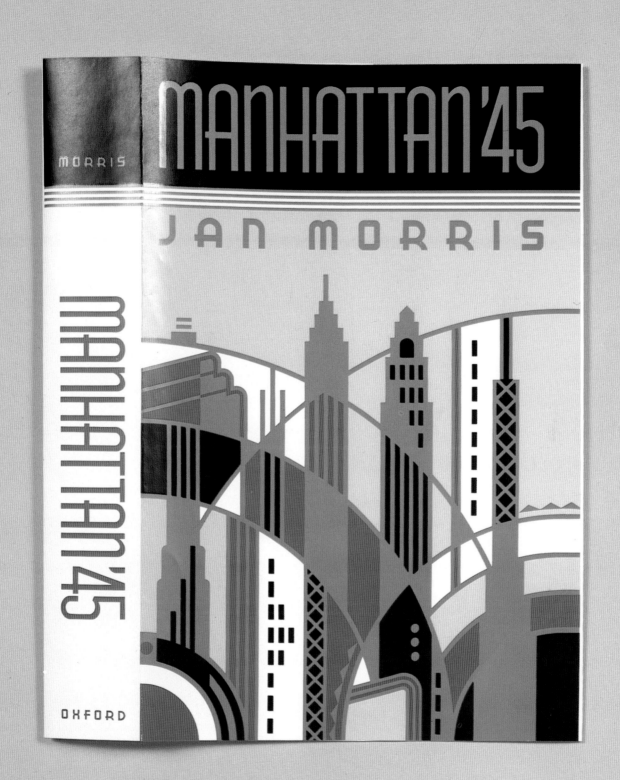

BOOK JACKET
TYPOGRAPHY/DESIGN *Daniel Pelavin, New York, New York* **LETTERER** *Daniel Pelavin* **CLIENT** *Oxford University Press*
PRINCIPAL TYPE *Handlettering* **DIMENSIONS** *5½ × 8½ in. (14 × 21.6 cm).*

SEVEN DAYS OF FELLOWSHIP WITH
INSIGHT FOR LIVING AND CHUCK SWINDOLL

· PORTS OF CALL ·

· ACCOMMODATIONS ·

· REGISTRATION ·

July 24–31, 1986

INVITATION
TYPOGRAPHY/DESIGN *Michael Standlee, Newport Beach, California* **CALLIGRAPHER** *Michael Standlee* **STUDIO** *Michael Standlee Design, Inc.* **CLIENT** *Insight for Living* **DIMENSIONS** *9 × 4 in. (22.9 × 10.2 cm).*

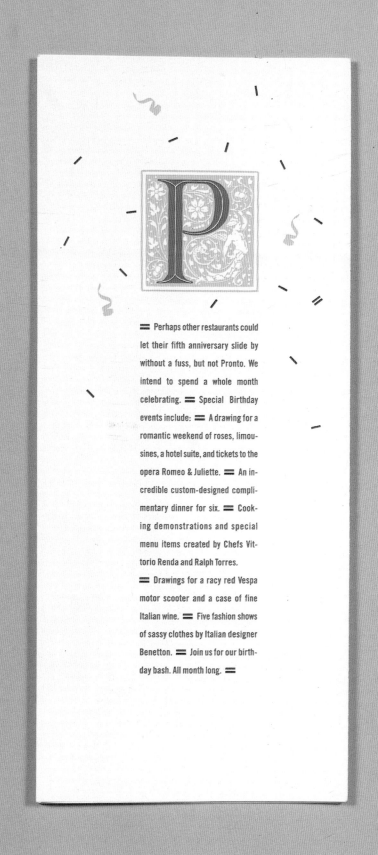

ANNOUNCEMENT

TYPOGRAPHY/DESIGN *Bob Goebel, Kevin B. Kuester, and Eric Madsen, Minneapolis, Minnesota* TYPOGRAPHIC SUPPLIER *Typeshooters, Inc.* STUDIO *Madsen and Kuester, Inc.* CLIENT *Parasole Restaurant Holdings, Inc.* PRINCIPAL TYPE *Franklin Extra Condensed* DIMENSIONS *10¼ × 30⅝ in. (26 × 78 cm).*

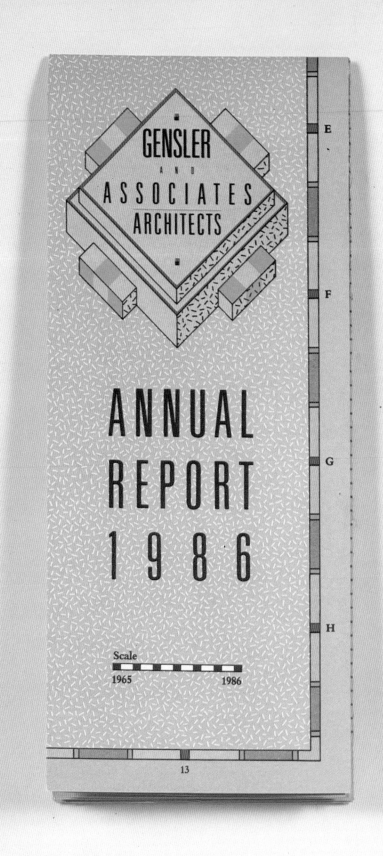

ANNUAL REPORT
TYPOGRAPHY/DESIGN *John Bricker, Susan Hopper, and Barbara Leistico, San Francisco, California* **TYPOGRAPHIC SUPPLIER** *Mercury Typography, Inc.* **STUDIO** *Gensler Graphics Group* **CLIENT** *Gensler & Associates/Architects* **PRINCIPAL TYPES** *Bembo (text) and Univers 29 (heads)* **DIMENSIONS** *26 × 18 in. (66 × 46 cm).*

It's time for a station break.

CORPORATE IDENTITY
TYPOGRAPHY/DESIGN *Steve Snider, Wellesley, Massachusetts* **LETTERER** *Steve Snider* **TYPOGRAPHIC SUPPLIER** *Rand Typography*
AGENCY *Rossin, Greenberg, Seronick & Hill* **CLIENT** *WHCT-18, Hartford* **PRINCIPAL TYPE** *Handlettering* **DIMENSIONS** *Various.*

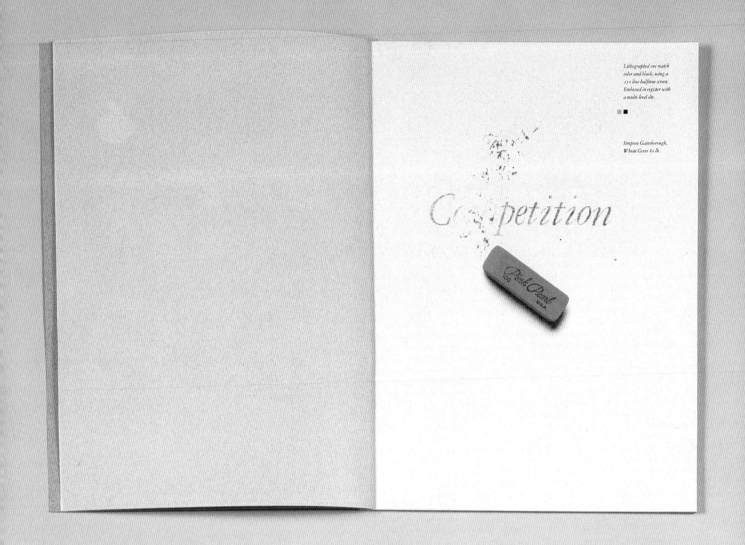

BROCHURE
TYPOGRAPHY/DESIGN *Michael Skjei, San Francisco, California* **TYPOGRAPHIC SUPPLIER** *Mackenzie-Harris* **STUDIO** *Cross Associates*
CLIENT *Simpson Paper Company* **PRINCIPAL TYPE** *Garamond No. 4* **DIMENSIONS** *9 × 12 in. (22.8 × 30.5 cm).*

POSTER
TYPOGRAPHY/DESIGN *Langfeld Associates, San Francisco, California* **TYPOGRAPHIC SUPPLIER** *Burch + McElroy Typographers*
STUDIO *Langfeld Associates* **CLIENT** *Langfeld Associates, Kathryn Kleinman, and Cannon Press* **PRINCIPAL TYPE** *Centaur*
DIMENSIONS *17½ × 26½ in. (44.5 × 67.3 cm).*

SERVICE

A TALK WITH TOM STEWART

Interview with Tom Stewart

Tom Stewart took over as President and Chief Executive Officer of Tradewell Group in June of this year. Since then many changes have taken place within the organization. More changes are anticipated as Tom and his new management team work to restore Tradewell, PriceSetter and Prairie Markets stores' reputation as the industry leader in customer service and satisfaction.

Tom remains Chief Executive Officer of Services Group of America, a holding company which manages Storedining Services of America, Miller Cascade, Eagle Pacific Insurance and Pacific Gamble Robinson. Tom and SGA President Ricky Smith have led the company through a period of rapid expansion and diversification. Founded in 1981 as Seattle Storedine Company, the company began its real growth during the period between 1984 and 1990 as

it acquired ten different companies located in ports throughout Washington. It purchased Miller Produce in 1972 and United Cascade Foods in 1974.

Tom Stewart came onboard full time in 1967 after graduating from the University of Washington with a degree in accounting. With Tom and Ricky at the helm, the company has continued its growth and diversification. The success has always been based upon their ability to attract and keep good people and in having those people provide the highest level of service possible to their customers. That emphasis on service will continue to be the foundation of Tom's efforts at Tradewell.

M.R.: Tom, soon after it was announced Miller Cascade had acquired Pacific Gamble Robinson, the rumors were Tradewell, Prairie Market and PriceSetter stores would be sold. Why didn't you sell?

Stewart: "We did receive some offers for the stores right after we acquired them, but in looking at the situation we felt there was too great an opportunity at Tradewell for us to sell them. At that time, we weren't familiar with the retail grocery business, but we realized the offers we were receiving weren't equal to the value we felt the company has. We were impressed with the numbers and after close examination came to the realization that with the right moves, this company could be quickly restored to a profitable position. So, we made the decision to keep them, and now that we have, we're in the game to stay. Two years down the road, our competitors will wish they had paid us three times what they offered."

M.R.: What kind of support will you be providing the stores?

Stewart: "Basically we're going to allow the individual store managers to do their own jobs. We'll provide them with the tools necessary to perform and to respond to the individual needs in the neighborhoods they serve, and we'll stay out of their way. That doesn't mean they won't hear from us, because they will. We want them all to meet our goals for service and profit and we'll be working with them to ensure they can succeed."

This first issue of *Market Report* is dedicated to the service level we will be providing our customers. The line, "Nobody Provides Better Service, Nobody!" is intended as an in-house promotional theme, but it could become a part of the company's advertising and other public communications.

Just what exactly does it mean? What will the customer come to expect in terms of service when they shop at our stores?

Tom Stewart, President and Chief Executive Officer, puts it very simply. He says, "It is my intention for the Tradewell Group to raise the level of customer service and satisfaction to the highest mark in the retail food service industry."

Stewart recently provided each manager with a copy of the best selling book "In Search of Excellence." In his letter to the managers which accompanied the book he said, "Today's business environment and corporate objectives are driven by addressing customers' needs. We are no longer an industrial society. We are in a service era and the company which provides the best service at the best price to each of its customers will become the industry leader. Period."

Stewart is right. America today is based upon a service economy. The key to providing top and quality service is people. As Andrew Carnegie once said, "Take my people and leave my factories soon grass will grow through the cracks on the floor. Take my factories and leave my people, and soon I will have bigger and better factories."

The secret of success for the companies of Services Group of America is the ability to motivate and keep good people. No matter what problem a customer faces, SGA will find a solution to that problem immediately.

"We constantly try to put ourselves in the customer's shoes," explains Stewart, "in order to see a problem through their eyes. In that way we can be in the best position to completely answer their needs."

NOBODY PROVIDES BETTER SERVICE NOBODY

The Tradewell Group will be rebuilt by providing this same approach to our customers. The over-riding goal of Tradewell is to have every customer personally satisfied by their experience. In order to achieve that goal, each Tradewell employee must strive to:

Take a personal interest in each customer who enters your store. That means taking the time to get to know the repeat customers. Helping with their groceries. Helping

them find a special item. Smiling at the customers and welcoming them to your store, because it is your store.

Giving extra effort to the customer while they are in the store. If a customer looks as though they cannot find an item, offer to assist them. Or, if you pass a customer, say "hi" and make sure they have everything they need. If they need special packing of meat, or other items, gladly respond to the request. Ask the customer for input on the items carried in the store and what kinds of new items or brands they would like carried.

Participate in the Tradewell Team by taking a personal interest in your fellow employees. Each and every Tradewell team member plays an important role in our ultimate success. If one customer in one store is offended by the actions of one team member, the customer will take their business to the competition. You can bet on it. On the other hand, if one customer is impressed by your personal attention to them and that of your fellow team members, they will come back and the chances are good that they will bring new customers with them. Feel good about what you are doing and it will show.

Always remember that the customer is right. We are all employed for one reason only - that is to serve the needs of the customer. We must be dedicated to providing them the very best service available anywhere or they simply will not return to our store. We cannot promote one thing and deliver something else.

Take Pride in Your Job. Remember that each and every job within the Tradewell Group is an important one because it's an integral part of the overall service we provide our customers. Don't think that because you don't have a great deal of contact with the customer that it is unimportant for you to smile or welcome them into your store. It is. Every person who works for us makes an impression upon the customer while they are visiting our store. We want that impression to be a positive one. Show you are proud of your job and your store. Project confidence.

"The quality of service to the customer will not come from the planned improvements to our stores, or through the consolidation of stores, but rather by an effort of each team member on a one-to-one relationship with each and every one of our customers," Stewart said. "The store improvements will help but not nearly as much as the individual effort of each Tradewell group employee taking a personal interest in their customer."

Service is our paramount concern. It's number one in importance.

NEWSLETTER

TYPOGRAPHY/DESIGN *Jack Anderson and Luann Bice, Seattle, Washington* **TYPOGRAPHIC SUPPLIER** *Thomas & Kennedy/Type House* **STUDIO** *Hornall Anderson Design Works* **CLIENT** *Tradewell Group* **PRINCIPAL TYPES** *Bodoni Antiqua Bold Condensed and Bodoni Book* **DIMENSIONS** *11 × 17 in. (27.9 × 43.2 cm).*

POSTER
TYPOGRAPHY/DESIGN *Michelle Beckhardt-Lada, New York, New York* **TYPOGRAPHIC SUPPLIER** *In-house* **AGENCY** *Bruce McGaw Graphics*
PRINCIPAL TYPE *Helvetica* **DIMENSIONS** *36 × 26 in. (91.4 × 66 cm).*

PACKAGING
TYPOGRAPHY/DESIGN *Mark Galarneau, Palo Alto, California* **TYPOGRAPHIC SUPPLIER** *Context* **AGENCY** *Darien & Morra/Galarneau & Sinn, Ltd.* **CLIENT** *Accolade* **PRINCIPAL TYPE** *ITC Cheltenham Light* **DIMENSIONS** *8³⁄₄ × 8³⁄₄ in. (22.3 × 22.3 cm).*

CALENDAR
TYPOGRAPHY/DESIGN *Carole Bouchard, Boston, Massachusetts* **TYPOGRAPHIC SUPPLIER** *Typographic House* **AGENCY** *HBM/Creamer, Inc.*
STUDIO *HBM/Creamer Design Group* **CLIENT** *General Electric Plastics* **PRINCIPAL TYPE** *Gill Sans SCT* **DIMENSIONS** *10 × 11 in.*
(25.4 × 27.9 cm).

BOOKLET
TYPOGRAPHY/DESIGN *Hermann Rapp, Weilrod, West Germany* **CALLIGRAPHER** *Hermann Rapp* **TYPOGRAPHIC SUPPLIER** *Fotosatz Hoffmann* **STUDIO** *Bölling, Offizin für Prägedruck* **CLIENT** *Bölling, Offizin für Prägedruck* **PRINCIPAL TYPE** *Joanna* **DIMENSIONS** *7³⁄₈ × 11⁷⁄₈ in. (10.7 × 30.1 cm).*

CATALOG
TYPOGRAPHY/DESIGN *Robert Cipriani, Boston, Massachusetts* **TYPOGRAPHIC SUPPLIER** *Wrightson Typographers* **AGENCY** *Cipriani Advertising, Inc.* **CLIENT** *Cole-Haan* **PRINCIPAL TYPE** *ITC New Baskerville* **DIMENSIONS** *9 × 12 in. (23 × 30.5 cm).*

BROCHURE
TYPOGRAPHY/DESIGN *Alan Peckolick, New York, New York* **TYPOGRAPHIC SUPPLIER** *Cardinal Type Service, Inc.* **AGENCY** *Peckolick & Partners* **STUDIO** *Peckolick & Partners* **CLIENT** *General Electric Venture Capital Corporation* **PRINCIPAL TYPE** *Cheltenham Light Condensed* **DIMENSIONS** *8½ × 11 in. (21.6 × 27.9 cm).*

· STATIONERY
TYPOGRAPHY/DESIGN *Craig Frazier, San Francisco, California* **CALLIGRAPHER** *Georgia Deaver, San Francisco, California*
TYPOGRAPHIC SUPPLIER *Display Lettering & Copy* **STUDIO** *Frazier Design* **CLIENT** *E Street Restaurant* **PRINCIPAL TYPE** *ITC Garamond Book Condensed* **DIMENSIONS** *8½ × 11 in. (21.6 × 27.9 cm).*

Thales of Miletus, one of the fathers of Greek philosophy, founded his school of thought on the premise: "All things are water." Twenty-five hundred years later, nothing has changed in the world to diminish the place and importance of water. It is at the heart of all industries and essential to Potlatch.

Throughout Potlatch's 82-year history, water and the company's successful growth have been inextricably interwoven. In our forests, photosynthesis, the activity that ultimately makes life in the forest and elsewhere possible, would be extremely difficult without the key role played by water.

Rushing rivers in Idaho and Minnesota, and the log drives they sustained for decades,

Northern Idaho's Lake Coeur d'Alene performs an important dual role as a transportation link for Potlatch raw materials and as a log storage facility for the Rutledge unit sawmill.

epitomized one of the most colorful and exciting chapters in Potlatch history. Since then, man-made changes in waterways near our operations have helped create major gateways to world markets for Potlatch products.

Many Potlatch plants were built on rivers or lakes that provided low-cost power, log storage and transportation of supplies and finished goods. Lewiston at the confluence of the Snake and Clearwater, major tributaries

of the Columbia; Brainerd on the Mississippi and Cloquet on the St. Louis rivers in northern Minnesota; and Cypress Bend several hundred miles farther south on the Mississippi River in Arkansas, are examples of major Potlatch mill sites that owe their existence to water.

In early Potlatch mills, steam was used to power lumber saws and waterwheels ran stone pulpwood grinders. Today, huge quantities of water are essential to Potlatch operations throughout the country.

The proper management of this resource in our forests, for transportation, manufacturing or power, and in the environment, remains vitally important to the company's future growth.

Water

Water is the common denominator of every living thing on earth. Reverently described by some as "Adam's ale," the world's appreciation for this precious resource is boundless. This is our story of how we use and respect water's many qualities in all of our activities.

Minnesota boasts the largest area of water among Potlatch states. Its 12,000-plus lakes and 25,000 miles of rivers cover six percent of the entire state.

From its beginning in New England, the river drive was repeated across the U.S. for more than 200 years. Furious white-water was a constant danger. Potlatch ran the last major log drive in the nation on Idaho's Clearwater river in 1971. Charles "Red" McCollister, now retired in Omlmo, supervised Clearwater log drives for 15 years.

ANNUAL REPORT
TYPOGRAPHY/DESIGN *Kit Hinrichs, San Francisco, California* **TYPOGRAPHIC SUPPLIER** *Reardon & Krebs* **STUDIO** *Pentagram*
CLIENT *Potlatch Corporation* **PRINCIPAL TYPE** *Times Roman* **DIMENSIONS** *8½ × 11 in. (21.6 × 27.9 cm).*

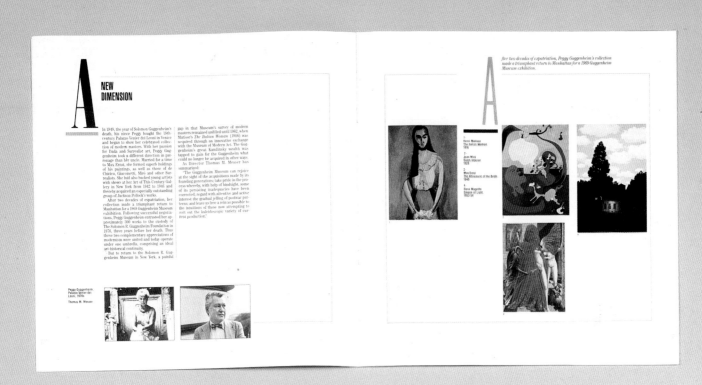

A NEW DIMENSION

In 1949, the year of Solomon Guggenheim's death, his niece Peggy bought the 18th-century Palazzo Venier dei Leoni in Venice and began to show her celebrated collection of modern masters. With her passion for Dada and Surrealist art, Peggy Guggenheim took a different direction in patronage than her uncle. Married for a time to Max Ernst, she formed superb holdings of his paintings, as well as those of de Chirico, Giacometti, Miró and other Surrealists. She had also backed young artists with shows at her Art of This Century Gallery in New York from 1942 to 1946 and thereby acquired an especially outstanding group of Jackson Pollock's works.

After two decades of expatriation, her collection made a triumphant return to Manhattan for a 1969 Guggenheim Museum exhibition. Following successful negotiations, Peggy Guggenheim entrusted her approximately 300 works to the custody of The Solomon R. Guggenheim Foundation in 1976, three years before her death. Thus these two complementary appreciations of modernism were united and today operate under one umbrella, comprising an ideal art-historical continuity.

But to return to the Solomon R. Guggenheim Museum in New York, a painful gap in that Museum's survey of modern masters remained unfilled until 1982, when Matisse's *The Italian Woman* (1916) was acquired through an innovative exchange with the Museum of Modern Art. The Guggenheim's great Kandinsky wealth was tapped to gain for the Guggenheim what could no longer be acquired in other ways.

As Director Thomas M. Messer has summarized:

"The Guggenheim Museum can rejoice at the sight of the acquisitions made by its founding generations; take pride in the processes whereby, with help of hindsight, some of its persisting inadequacies have been corrected; regard with attentive and active interest the gradual jelling of postwar patterns; and leave as free a rein as possible to the intuitions of those now attempting to sort out the kaleidoscopic variety of current production."

Peggy Guggenheim,
Palazzo Venier dei
Leoni, 1970s.

Thomas M. Messer

fter two decades of expatriation, Peggy Guggenheim's collection made a triumphant return to Manhattan for a 1969 Guggenheim Museum exhibition.

1.
Henri Matisse
The Italian Woman
1916

2.
Jean Miró
Dutch Interior
1928

3.
Max Ernst
The Attirement of the Bride
1940

4.
Rene Magritte
Empire of Light
1953-54

BROCHURE
TYPOGRAPHY/DESIGN *Fausto Pellegrini, New York, New York* **TYPOGRAPHIC SUPPLIER** *Typologic* **AGENCY** *Jan Krukowski Associates*
CLIENT *The Guggenheim Museum* **PRINCIPAL TYPE** *Century Book Condensed* **DIMENSIONS** *11½ × 11½ in. (29 × 29 cm).*

CALENDAR
TYPOGRAPHY/DESIGN *Yoshihiro Yoshida, Shinjuku-ku, Tokyo, Japan* **CALLIGRAPHER** *Yoko Shindoh, Suginami-Ku, Tokyo, Japan*
TYPOGRAPHIC SUPPLIER *Robundo* **STUDIO** *Yoshihiro Yoshida Design Studio* **CLIENT** *Robundo* **PRINCIPAL TYPE** *Ryobi RMH-MR*
DIMENSIONS *11½ × 18 in. (29.2 × 45.7 cm).*

CALENDAR

TYPOGRAPHY/DESIGN *Pennor's, Paris, France* **CALLIGRAPHER** *Herve Rivoalland, Paris, France* **TYPOGRAPHIC SUPPLIER** *Face Photosetting* **CLIENT** *Face Photosetting* **PRINCIPAL TYPE** *ITC Century Light Condensed* **DIMENSIONS** *16½ × 23¼ in. (42 × 59 cm).*

The theme of this year's APL calendar is global trade and how the economic and cultural interdependence it creates has made our world grow smaller. Commerce has always mixed the economies and cultures of trading partners. When you see a new, white baseball or a colorful dragon kite, you may imagine the places and people that inspired them. Over the years, international travel and trade have allowed us to transport these symbols, and exchange, adapt, and absorb them according to our own needs. Baseball and sushi–although each is identified with a different culture–now enjoy international favor. However, the details of exporting these cultural and culinary elements can be complex. When we see how many nations contribute their products to the manufacture of a baseball, or the far-flung efforts required to produce a string of cultured pearls, we realize how much these cross-pollinations depend on trade. Trade enriches us economically and culturally, and we invite you to enjoy our celebration of that fact in words and images throughout the year.

American President Lines
1987 Calendar

CALENDAR
TYPOGRAPHY/DESIGN *Kit Hinrichs, San Francisco, California* **TYPOGRAPHIC SUPPLIER** *Reardon & Krebs* **STUDIO** *Pentagram*
CLIENT *American President Companies* **PRINCIPAL TYPE** *Times Roman* **DIMENSIONS** *16 × 25 in. (40.6 × 63.5 cm).*

Monogramas Cópirraite: Miran

INVITATION
TYPOGRAPHY/DESIGN *Georgia Deaver, San Francisco, California* **CALLIGRAPHER** *Georgia Deaver* **STUDIO** *Georgia Deaver Calligraphy and Handlettering* **DIMENSIONS** *5¹/₄ × 7⁷/₈ in. (13.3 × 20 cm).*

LOGOTYPE
TYPOGRAPHY/DESIGN *Robert Miles Runyan, Playa Del Rey, California* **CREATIVE DIRECTOR** *Vanig Torikian* **STUDIO** *Robert Miles Runyan & Associates* **CLIENT** *L.A. Heat Soccer Team* **PRINCIPAL TYPE** *Handlettering.*

POSTER
TYPOGRAPHY/DESIGN *Randall Sexton, San Jose, California* **LETTERER** *Randall Sexton* **TYPOGRAPHIC SUPPLIER** *LaserType*
STUDIO *IBM Design Center* **CLIENT** *IBM Club San Jose* **PRINCIPAL TYPE** *Helvetica* **DIMENSIONS** *15 × 21 in. (38 × 53 cm).*

The
Harris
County
Medical
Society
Reports:

THE
Liabil_.ty
CRISIS
IN TEXAS

MAGAZINE
TYPOGRAPHY/DESIGN *Monica Keogh, Houston, Texas* **TYPOGRAPHIC SUPPLIER** *Graphics Plus* **STUDIO** *Monica Keogh Design*
CLIENT *The Harris County Medical Society* **PRINCIPAL TYPE** *Futura* **DIMENSIONS** *8½ × 11 in. (21.6 × 27.9 cm).*

LOGOTYPE
TYPOGRAPHY/DESIGN *Mark Galarneau, Palo Alto, California* **LETTERER** *Mark Galarneau* **AGENCY** *Galarneau & Sinn, Ltd.*
CLIENT *Art Directors Heaven* **PRINCIPAL TYPE** *ITC Avant Garde.*

ADVERTISEMENT
TYPOGRAPHY/DESIGN *Tony Sauvage, Sydney, NSW, Australia* **TYPOGRAPHIC SUPPLIER** *Face, The Type Workshop* **AGENCY** *Saatchi & Saatchi Compton, Sydney* **CLIENT** *United Distillers Limited* **PRINCIPAL TYPE** *Centaur Light* **DIMENSIONS** *10¾ × 16¼ in. (27.5 × 41.5 cm).*

CHRISTMAS GREETING
TYPOGRAPHY/DESIGN *Charles Spencer Anderson, Minneapolis, Minnesota* **TYPOGRAPHIC SUPPLIER** *Typeshooters*
STUDIO *Duffy Design Group* **CLIENT** *Duffy Design Group* **PRINCIPAL TYPE** *Century Schoolbook*

CHRISTMAS CARD
TYPOGRAPHY/DESIGN *Leslie Hébert Helakoski, Pittsburgh, Pennsylvania* **TYPOGRAPHIC SUPPLIER** *Davis and Warde*
CLIENT *Leslie Hébert Helakoski* **PRINCIPAL TYPE** *Ronda Light* **DIMENSIONS** *6 × 4⅛ in. (15.2 × 10.5 cm).*

PACKAGING
TYPOGRAPHY/DESIGN *Amanda Finn, Toronto, Ontario, Canada* **TYPOGRAPHIC SUPPLIER** *Techni Process Lettering Limited*
STUDIO *Lawrence Finn and Associates Limited* **CLIENT** *Lawrence Finn and Associates Limited* **PRINCIPAL TYPE** *Snell Roundhand*
DIMENSIONS *3³⁄₈ × 5⁵⁄₈ in. (8.6 × 12.7 cm).*

GIFT BAG

TYPOGRAPHY/DESIGN *Lee Stork, Kansas City, Missouri* **CALLIGRAPHER** *Lee Stork* **CLIENT** *Ambassador Cards* **PRINCIPAL TYPE** *Handlettering*
DIMENSIONS *9 × 7 in. (22.9 × 17.9 cm).*

POSTER
TYPOGRAPHY/DESIGN *Colin Forbes and Maryann Levesque, New York, New York* **CALLIGRAPHER** *Paola, Age 7 (William Penn signature)* **TYPOGRAPHIC SUPPLIER** *Typogram* **CLIENT** *IBM* **PRINCIPAL TYPES** *Various* **DIMENSIONS** *8³⁄₄ × 12¹⁄₈ in. (22.2 × 30.7 cm).*

CHRISTMAS CARD
TYPOGRAPHY/DESIGN *Pat Sloan, Fort Worth, Texas* **CALLIGRAPHER** *Pat Sloan* **TYPOGRAPHIC SUPPLIER** *Fort Worth Linotyping Company, Inc.* **AGENCY** *Pat Sloan Design* **STUDIOS** *Bobalu Studios and Pat Sloan Design* **CLIENT** *Fort Worth Linotyping Company, Inc.* **PRINCIPAL TYPE** *Univers 57* **DIMENSIONS** *34½ × 8½ in. (87.6 × 21.6 cm).*

STATIONERY
TYPOGRAPHY/DESIGN *Sandra McHenry, San Francisco, California* **TYPOGRAPHIC SUPPLIER** *Spartan Typographers* **STUDIO** *Pentagram*
CLIENT *Mt. Everest Expedition* **PRINCIPAL TYPE** *Palatino* **DIMENSIONS** *8½ × 11 in. (21.6 × 27.9 cm).*

BROCHURE
TYPOGRAPHY/DESIGN *David Broom and Rich Newman, San Francisco, California* **TYPOGRAPHIC SUPPLIER** *City Type*
STUDIO *Broom & Broom, Inc.* **CLIENT** *The Bank of California* **PRINCIPAL TYPE** *Garamond* **DIMENSIONS** *9 × 11 in. (22.9 × 27.9 cm).*

MENU

TYPOGRAPHY/DESIGN *Robin Ayres, Dallas, Texas* **TYPOGRAPHIC SUPPLIER** *Southwestern Typographics* **AGENCY** *The Richards Group* **STUDIO** *Richards Brock Miller Mitchell and Associates* **CLIENT** *T.G.I. Friday's Inc.* **PRINCIPAL TYPES** *Franklin Gothic Condensed, Palatino (heads), and Palatino Italic (text)* **DIMENSIONS** *7½ × 12 in. (19 × 30.5 cm).*

ANNOUNCEMENT
TYPOGRAPHY/DESIGN *Rex Peteet and Walter Horton, Dallas, Texas* **CALLIGRAPHER** *Walter Horton and Rex Peteet*
TYPOGRAPHIC SUPPLIER *Southwestern Typographics* **STUDIO** *Sibley/Peteet Design, Inc.* **CLIENT** *International Paper Company*
PRINCIPAL TYPES *Rubens Extra Condensed, Serif Gothic, Futura Ultra Bold, Futura Medium, Microgramma Normal, Logothic Light, and New Gothic Condensed* **DIMENSIONS** *9½ × 13¼ in. (24.1 × 33.7 cm).*

RECORD ALBUM COVER
TYPOGRAPHY/DESIGN *Lisa Francella, New Rochelle, New York* **LETTERER** *Lisa Francella* **TYPOGRAPHIC SUPPLIER** *Photo-Lettering, Inc.*
STUDIO *Masoff & Scolnik Associates* **CLIENT** *Reader's Digest* **PRINCIPAL TYPES** *Empire, Atrax, and Bluejack Medium* **DIMENSIONS**
12 × 12 in. (30.5 × 30.5 cm).

STATIONERY
TYPOGRAPHY/DESIGN *Lindy Dunlavey, Sacramento, California* **ILLUSTRATOR** *Lindy Dunlavey* **TYPOGRAPHIC SUPPLIER** *Ad Type Graphics*
STUDIO *The Dunlavey Studio, Inc.* **CLIENT** *Java City Roasters* **PRINCIPAL TYPES** *Enviro (modified) and Futura Light and Medium*
Condensed **DIMENSIONS** *8½ × 11 in. (21.6 × 27.9 cm).*

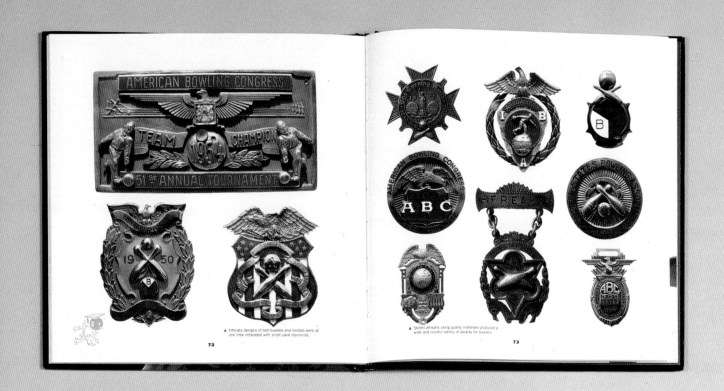

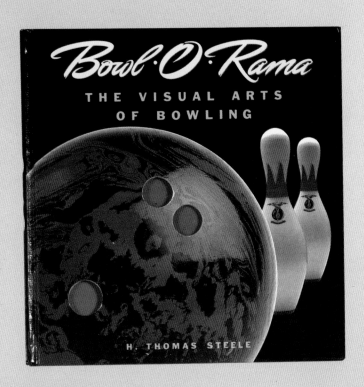

BOOK
TYPOGRAPHY/DESIGN *Tommy Steele, Los Angeles, California* **LETTERER** *Tommy Steele* **TYPOGRAPHIC SUPPLIERS** *New England Typographic Service and Characters & Color* **STUDIO** *SteeleWorks Design* **CLIENT** *Abbeville Press* **PRINCIPAL TYPES** *Franklin Gothic and Spire* **DIMENSIONS** *9 × 9 in. (22.9 × 22.9 cm).*

STATIONERY
TYPOGRAPHY/DESIGN *Lynne Shipman, Gill Fishman, and Tyler Smith, Cambridge, Massachusetts* **TYPOGRAPHIC SUPPLIER**
LithoComposition **STUDIO** *Gill Fishman Associates* **CLIENT** *Freedberg of Boston* **PRINCIPAL TYPE** *Gill Sans* **DIMENSIONS** *8½ × 11 in.*
(21.6 × 27.9 cm).

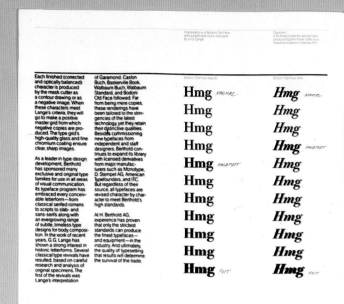

Interpretations of Bodoni Old Face
with weight selections indicated
by G.G. Lange

Opposite:
A finished character (actual size)
produced by the mask cutter as a
negative image on masking film

Each finished (corrected and optically balanced) character is produced by the mask cutter as a contour drawing or as a negative image. When these characters meet Lange's criteria, they will go to make a positive master grid from which negative copies are produced. The type grid's high-quality glass and fine chromium coating ensure clear, sharp images.

As a leader in type design development, Berthold has sponsored many exclusive and original type families for use in all areas of visual communication. Its typeface program has embraced every conceivable letterform—from classical serifed romans to scripts to slab- and sans-serifs along with an evergrowing range of subtle, timeless type designs for body composition. In the work of recent years, G.G. Lange has shown a strong interest in historic letterforms. Several classical type revivals have resulted, based on careful research and analysis of original specimens. The first of the revivals was Lange's interpretation

of Garamond, Caslon Buch, Baskerville Book, Walbaum Buch, Walbaum Standard, and Bodoni Old Face followed. Far from being mere copies, these renderings have been tailored to the stringencies of the latest technology, yet they retain their distinctive qualities. Besides commissioning new typefaces from independent and staff designers, Berthold continues to expand its library with licensed derivatives from major manufacturers such as Monotype, D. Stempel AG, American Typefounders, and ITC. But regardless of their source, all typefaces are revised character by character to meet Berthold's high standards.

At H. Berthold AG, experience has proven that only the strictest standards can produce the finest typefaces—and equipment—in the industry. And ultimately, the quality of typesetting that results will determine the survival of the trade.

Bodoni Old Face regular:

Bodoni Old Face italic:

NEWSLETTER

TYPOGRAPHY/DESIGN *Carl Wohlt, Chicago, Illinois* **TYPOGRAPHIC SUPPLIER** *Typographic Resource* **AGENCY** *Crosby Associates Inc.*
CLIENT *Typographic Resource* **PRINCIPAL TYPES** *Akzidenz-Grotesk Buch Light and Futura Extra Bold Condensed* **DIMENSIONS**
11³⁄₄ × 11³⁄₄ in. (30 × 30 cm).

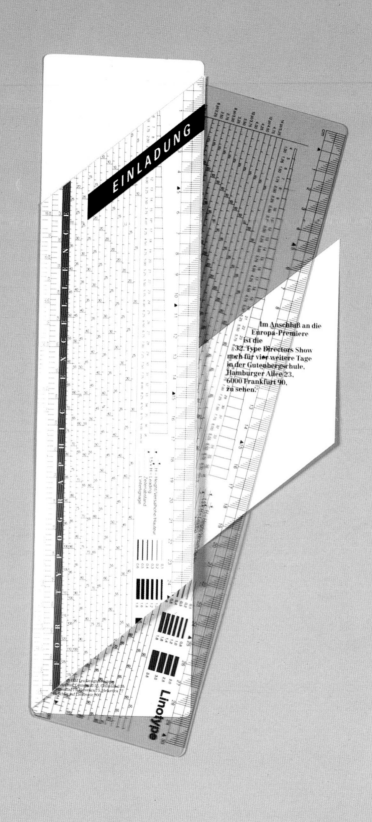

INVITATION
TYPOGRAPHY/DESIGN *Olaf Leu Design & Partner, Frankfurt, West Germany* **CALLIGRAPHER** *Olaf Leu Design & Partner*
TYPOGRAPHIC SUPPLIER *Con Composition/Mabo-Druck* **STUDIO** *Olaf Leu Design & Partner* **CLIENT** *Linotype GmbH* **PRINCIPAL TYPES**
Centennial Nos. 55, 56, 75 and Helvetica Nos. 75, 77 **DIMENSIONS** *4⅝ × 12⅞ in. (12 × 33 cm).*

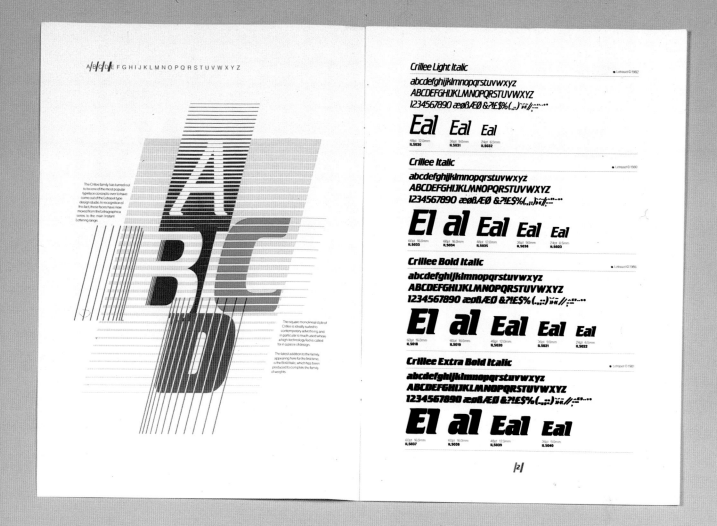

BROCHURE

TYPOGRAPHY/DESIGN *David Quay, London, England* **LETTERER** *Paul Gray, London, England* **TYPOGRAPHIC SUPPLIER** *Span Graphics Ltd.* **STUDIO** *Quay & Gray Design Consultants* **CLIENT** *Letraset UK Ltd.* **PRINCIPAL TYPE** *Helvetica Light* **DIMENSIONS** *8½ × 11¾ in. (21 × 29.7 cm).*

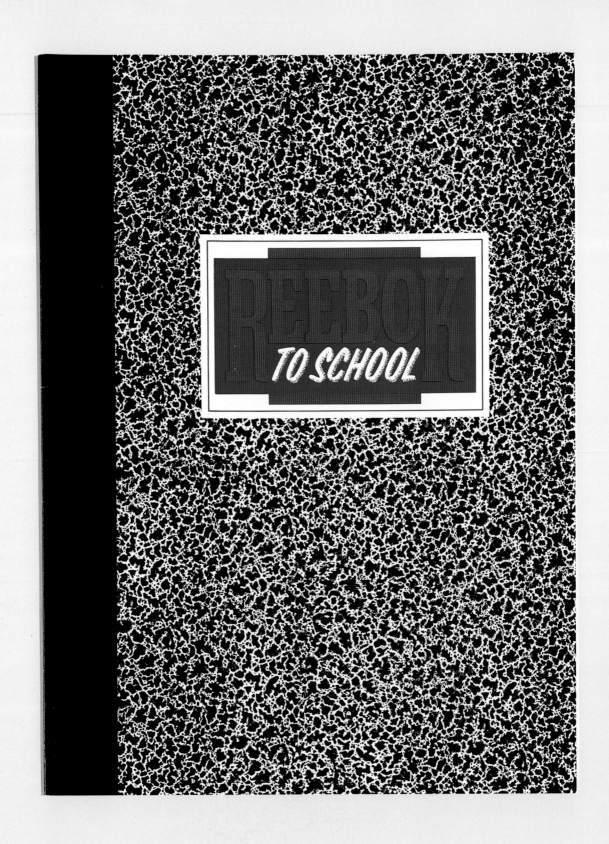

PROMOTIONAL FOLDER
TYPOGRAPHY/DESIGN *Steve Snider, Wellesley, Massachusetts* **CALLIGRAPHER** *Steve Snider* **TYPOGRAPHIC SUPPLIER** *Wrightson Typographers* **STUDIO** *Snider Design* **CLIENT** *Reebok International Ltd.* **DIMENSIONS** *9 × 12 in. (22.7 × 30.3 cm).*

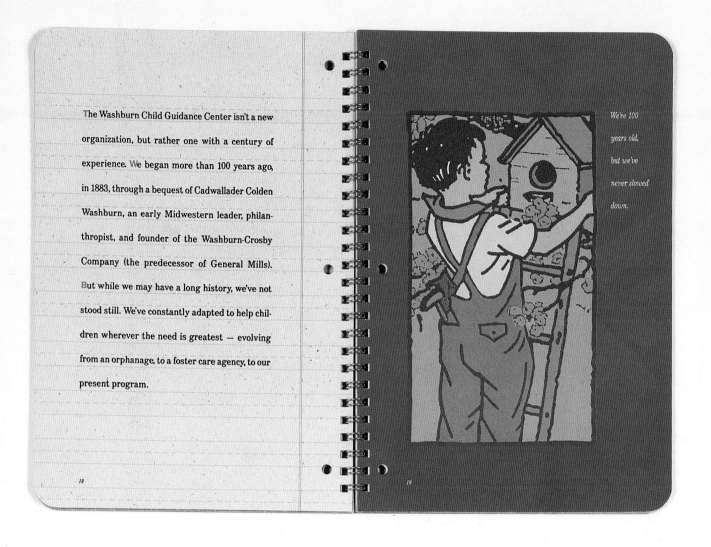

The Washburn Child Guidance Center isn't a new organization, but rather one with a century of experience. We began more than 100 years ago, in 1883, through a bequest of Cadwallader Colden Washburn, an early Midwestern leader, philanthropist, and founder of the Washburn-Crosby Company (the predecessor of General Mills). But while we may have a long history, we've not stood still. We've constantly adapted to help children wherever the need is greatest — evolving from an orphanage, to a foster care agency, to our present program.

We're 100 years old, but we've never slowed down.

BOOK
TYPOGRAPHY/DESIGN *Charles Spencer Anderson, Minneapolis, Minnesota* **TYPOGRAPHIC SUPPLIER** *Typeshooters* **STUDIO** *Duffy Design Group* **CLIENT** *Washburn Child Guidance Center* **PRINCIPAL TYPE** *Century Schoolbook* **DIMENSIONS** *6½ × 9¼ in. (16.5 × 23.5 cm).*

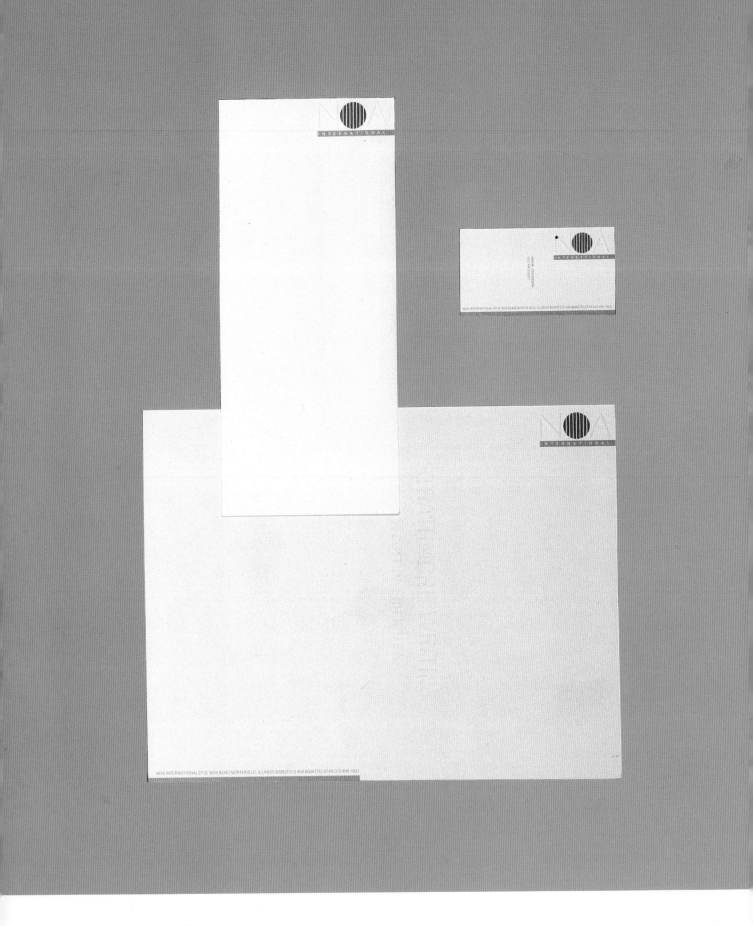

CORPORATE IDENTITY
TYPOGRAPHY/DESIGN *Kurt Meinecke, Chicago, Illinois* **TYPOGRAPHIC SUPPLIER** *Design Typographers* **STUDIO** *Group/Chicago*
CLIENT *NOA INTERNATIONAL, INC.* **PRINCIPAL TYPE** *Optima* **DIMENSIONS** *8½ × 11 in. (21.6 × 27.9 cm).*

STATIONERY
TYPOGRAPHY/DESIGN *Onofrio Paccione, New York, New York* **TYPOGRAPHIC SUPPLIER** *Typographics Plus Inc.*
STUDIO *TSI Communications* **CLIENT** *TSI Communications* **PRINCIPAL TYPES** *Helvetica Medium and Avant Garde Book*
DIMENSIONS *8½×11 in. (21.6×27.9 cm).*

STATIONERY

TYPOGRAPHY/DESIGN *Lisa Halperin, New York, New York* **LETTERER** *Ed Benguiat, New York, New York* **TYPOGRAPHIC SUPPLIER**
Photo-Lettering, Inc. **CLIENT** *Lisa Halperin* **PRINCIPAL TYPE** *ITC Newtext Regular* **DIMENSIONS** *8½ × 11 in. (21.6 × 27.9 cm).*

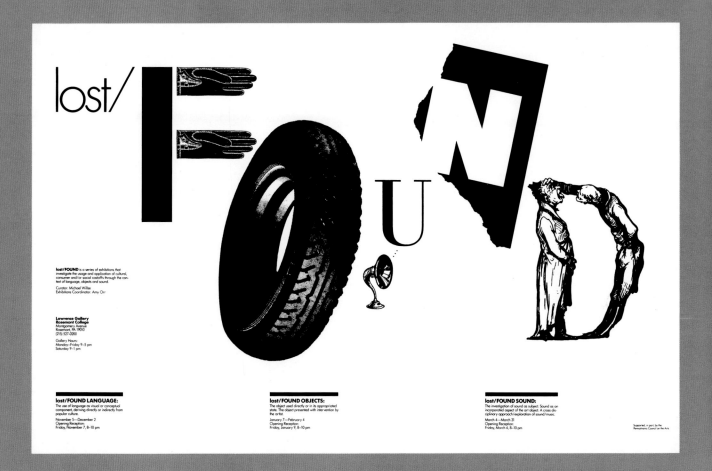

POSTER
TYPOGRAPHY/DESIGN *Joe Scorsone, Wyncote, Pennsylvania* **TYPOGRAPHIC SUPPLIER** *John C. Meyer* **STUDIO** *Scorsone/Drueding*
CLIENT *Rosemont College* **PRINCIPAL TYPE** *Futura* **DIMENSIONS** *30 × 20 in. (76.2 × 50.8 cm).*

QUALITY.

What should you look for first? The easy answer: quality. But what does quality mean to you? Is it what you tell your friends when you choose a college? Or what you've become when you leave it? To some people, academic quality means burying themselves in the books. To others, it means getting hands-on experience in a chosen field. ❦ Many people see quality in a large university. In the research interests of professors and graduate students. In lectures given by a prestigious professor; it may not matter if he knows who you are. In the excitement of sharing a stadium with 25,000 cheering fans. ❦ Others see it in a small college. In the personal attention a professor pays to undergraduates. In a teacher who joins her students for a cup of coffee to continue the discussion they began in class. In the chance to play, or to root for the home team along with 2,500 people, most of whom you recognize. ❦ Certainly, one key should be strong programs in areas that interest you, and a range of choices wide enough to let you change your mind. Another good measure is the kind of careers graduates pursue, and how well the college prepares them. ❦ Quality can mean many things. Chances are, the school that combines the right qualities for you is a rare one. You have to look for it. Visit several college campuses. Talk to professors and students. Sit in on a class or two. But first, figure out the right questions to ask. ❦ Remember, quality is an individual matter. Only you can decide what it means to you.

If your idea of a quality education is a college small enough to make you feel at home, but large enough to offer you a wide range of opportunities; a school where professors are committed to teaching, where students can gain real-world experience in their fields, where graduates embark on successful careers; a public institution that feels a lot like a private one; you should look into Shepherd.

A community of 2,100 full-time undergraduates and 1,700 part-time students, Shepherd strikes an uncommon balance between the warmth and friendliness of a small college and the broad offerings of a larger institution. The average class has only 20 to 25 students. And there are 70 programs of study from accounting to engineering, from art to education to park administration.

How to choose the right college? Choose Shepherd.

At Shepherd, you'll never have to learn from graduate teaching assistants. All classes are taught by Shepherd professors, most of whom hold the most advanced degrees in their fields.

"Professors really care about their students," says one recent graduate, "about teaching them and about helping them get started with their careers."

For more information about Shepherd College, return the enclosed reply card. Give the other card to a friend!

To learn more about Shepherd return the enclosed card.

BROCHURE
TYPOGRAPHY/DESIGN *Scott J. Ward, Baltimore, Maryland* **TYPOGRAPHIC SUPPLIERS** *B.G. Composition and Phil's Photo*
AGENCY *Barton-Gillet* **CLIENT** *Shepherd College* **PRINCIPAL TYPE** *Cloister* **DIMENSIONS** *8½ × 11 in. (21.6 × 27.9 cm).*

STADTTHEATER | KONSTANZ | SPIELZEIT | 1986 | 87

„THEATER IN KONSTANZ"

BROCHURE
TYPOGRAPHY/DESIGN *Peter Horlacher, Stuttgart/Baden-Württemberg, West Germany* **TYPOGRAPHIC SUPPLIER** *Druckerei Pfeffer*
STUDIO *Peter Horlacher, Graphic und Photo-Design* **CLIENT** *Stadttheater Konstanz* **PRINCIPAL TYPE** *Serifa* **DIMENSIONS** *8¼ × 11¾ in.*
(21 × 29.7 cm).

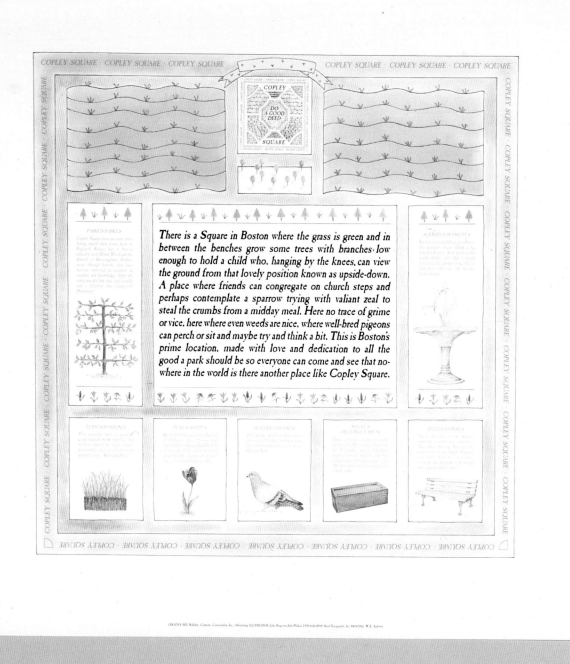

POSTER

TYPOGRAPHY/DESIGN *Andreé Cordella, Boston, Massachusetts* **TYPOGRAPHIC SUPPLIER** *Typographic House* **AGENCY** *Hill, Holliday/Design*
CLIENT *Copley Square Centennial Committee* **PRINCIPAL TYPE** *Caslon Antique Oblique* **DIMENSIONS** *23 × 23 in. (58.4 × 58.4 cm).*

CALL FOR ENTRIES FOR TYPOGRAPHY 8/TDC 33 *Design by David Brier.*

TYPE DIRECTORS CLUB

OFFICERS

President	John Luke
Vice President	Jack Odette
Secretary/Treasurer	Ed Benguiat
Directors-at-Large	Roger Black
	Leon Ettinger
	Blanche Fiorenza
	Allan Haley
	Edward A. Hamilton
	Minoru Morita
	Richard F. Mullen
Chairperson, Board of Directors	Klaus Schmidt

COMMITTEE FOR TDC 33

Chairperson	Ed Benguiat
Designer	David Brier
Coordinator	Carol Wahler
Printer	Potomac Graphic Industries, Inc.
Calligrapher	Robert Boyajian
Staff Photographer	Richard Mullen
Receiving Facilities	Cardinal Type Service, Inc.
Assistants to Judges	Godfrey Biscardi, John Bomparte,
	Laurie Burns, Penny Ellis,
	Blanche Fiorenza, Holley Flagg,
	Lisa Halperin, John Luke,
	Marilyn Marcus, Adolfo Martinez,
	Minoru Morita, Luther Parson,
	Dirk Rowntree, Klaus Schmidt,
	Victor Spindler, Walter Stanton,
	Lucile Tuttle-Smith, Edward N. Vadala,
	Allan R. Wahler

TYPE DIRECTORS CLUB
60 East 42nd Street
Suite 1130
New York, NY 10165
212-983-6042
Carol Wahler, Executive Director

INTERNATIONAL LIAISON CHAIRPERSONS

Ernst Dernehl
Dernehl & Dernehl
Design Consultants
Box 150 60
S-400 41 Göteborg
SWEDEN

Japan Typography Association
Kanamori Bldg. 4th Floor
12-9, Sendagaya 1-chome
Shibuya-ku, Tokyo 151
JAPAN

Jean Larcher
16 Chemin des Bourgognes
95000 Cergy
FRANCE

Professor Olaf Leu
Olaf Leu Design & Partner
Leipziger Str. 3
D-6000 Frankfurt am Main 90
WEST GERMANY

Oswaldo Miranda (Miran)
Av. Centenario, 2000
Curitiba—PR
80.000 BRAZIL

Keith Murgatroyd
Royle Murgatroyd
Design Associates Limited
24/41 Wenlock Road
London N1 7SR
ENGLAND

Simon Pemberton
Type Directors Club
45 Hale Road
Mosman, Sydney, N.S.W. 2000
AUSTRALIA

STV/AST
Swiss Typographic Association
Bahnhofweg 6
CH-8157 Dielsdorf
SWITZERLAND

*For membership information please contact
the Type Directors Club office.*

MEMBERSHIP

George Abrams '71
Mary Margaret Ahern '83
Leonard F. Bahr '62
Peter Bain '86
Don Baird '69
Gladys Barton '83
Clarence Baylis '74
Edward Benguiat '64
Peter Bertolami '69
Emil Biemann '75
Godfrey Biscardi '70
Roger Black '80
Sharon Blume '86
Art Boden '77
Karl Heinz Boelling '86
Friedrich Georg Boes '67
Garrett Boge '83
David Brier '81
Ed Brodsky '80
Kathie Brown '84
William Brown '84
Werner Brudi '66
Bernard Brussel-Smith* '47
Bill Bundzak '64
Aaron Burns '54
John Burton '85
Joseph Buscemi '82
Daniel Canter '82
Tom Carnase '73
Younghee Choi '86
Alan Christie '77
Robert Cipriani '85
Travis Cliett '53
Mahlon A. Cline '48
Elaine Coburn '85
Tom Cocozza '76
Barbara Cohen '85
Ed Colker '83
Freeman Craw* '47
James Cross '61
Ray Cruz '75
David Cundy '85
Derek Dalton '82
Susan Darbyshire '87
Ismar David '58
Whedon Davis '67
Saundra De Geneste '85
Cosimo De Maglie '74
Robert Defrin '69
Claude Dieterich '84
Ralph Di Meglio '74
Lou Dorfsman '54
Constance Doyle '86
John Dreyfus** '68
Christopher Dubber '85
William Duevell '80
Curtis Dwyer '78
Rick Eiber '85
Lee Einzig '85
Penny Ellis '84
Joseph Michael Essex '78
Eugene Ettenberg* '47
Leon Ettinger '84
Bob Farber '58
Sidney Feinberg '49
Joseph A. Fielder '83
Amanda Finn '87
Lawrence Finn '87
Blanche Fiorenza '82
Holley Flagg '81

Norbert Florendo '84
Glenn Foss* '47
Dean Franklin '80
Elizabeth Frenchman '83
Adrian Frutiger** '67
David Gatti '81
Stuart Germain '74
John Gibson '84
Lou Glassheim* '47
Howard Glener '77
Jeff Gold '84
Alan Gorelick '85
Edward Gottschall '52
Norman Graber '69
Diana Graham '85
Austin Grandjean '59
Kurt Haiman '82
Allan Haley '78
Edward A. Hamilton '83
Mark L. Handler '83
William Paul Harkins '83
Sherri Harnick '83
Horace Hart '67
Knut Hartmann '85
Carolyn Hawks '85
Geoffrey Hayes '86
Bonnie Hazelton '75
Carol Heiser '87
Fritz Hofrichter '80
Gerard Huerta '85
Donald Jackson** '78
Mary Jaquier '77
Allen Johnston '74
R. W. Jones '64
Judith Teener Kahn '85
R. Randolph Karch* '47
Rachel Katzen '81
Louis Kelley '84
Michael O. Kelly '80
Scott Kelly '84
Alice Kenny '85
Tom Kerrigan '77
Lawrence Kessler '63
Zoltan Kiss '59
Robert Knecht '69
Tom Knights '85
Steve Kopec '74
Linda Kosarin '83
Gene Krackehl '75
Bernhard J. Kress '63
Walter M. Kryshak '84
James Laird '69
Guenter Gerhard Lange '83
Jean Larcher '81
Mo Lebowitz '61
Arthur B. Lee* '47
Judith Kazdym Leeds '83
Louis Lepis '84
Professor Olaf Leu '66
Mark Lichtenstein '84
Clifton Line '51
Wally Littman '60
Sergio Liuzzi '85
John Howland Lord* '47
John Luke '78
Ed Malecki '59
Sol Malkoff '63
Marilyn Marcus '79
Stanley Markocki '71
John S. Marmaras '78

Frank B. Marshall III '78
Adolfo Martinez '86
Rogério Martins '85
Donna Marxer '85
James Mason '80
Les Mason '85
Jack Matera '73
John Matt '82
Fernando Medina '78
Professor Frédéric Metz '85
Douglas Michalek '77
John Milligan '78
Michael Miranda '84
Oswaldo Miranda '78
Barbara Montgomery '78
Richard Moore '82
Ronald Morganstein '77
Minoru Morita '75
Patti Morrone '85
Tobias Moss* '47
Erik Murphy '85
Richard Mullen '82
Keith Murgatroyd '78
Louis A. Musto '65
Alexander Nesbitt '50
Paschoal Fabra Neto '85
Alexa Nosal '87
Jan Allan Nowak '85
Josanne Nowak '86
Jack Odette '77
Thomas D. Ohmer '77
Motoaki Okuizumi '78
Brian O'Neill '68
Gerard J. O'Neill* '47
Jane Opiat '84
Vincent Pacella '83
Zlata W. Paces '78
Bob Paganucci '85
Luther Parson '82
Charles Pasewark '81
Eugene Pattberg* '47
Alan Peckolick '86
B. Martin Pedersen '85
Robert Peters '86
Roma Plakyda '80
Roy Podorson '77
Louis Portuesi '67
Richard Puder '85
David Quay '80
Elissa Querzé '83
Erwin Raith '67
Adeir Rampasso '85
Paul Rand** '86
Hermann Rapp '87
John Rea '82
Bud Renshaw '83
Jack Robinson '64
Edward Rondthaler* '47
Robert M. Rose '77
Herbert M. Rosenthal '62
Tom Roth '85
Dirk Rowntree '86
Joseph E. Rubino '83
Erkki Ruuhinen '86
Gus Saelens '50
Bob Salpeter '68
David Saltman '66
John N. Schaedler '63
Hermann J. Schlieper '87
Hermann Schmidt '83

Klaus Schmidt '59
Werner Schneider '87
Eileen Hedy Schultz '85
Eckehart Schumacher-Gebler '85
Robert Scott '84
Michael G. Scotto '82
David Seager '85
William L. Sekuler* '47
Ellen Shapiro '85
Mark Simkins '86
Jerry Singleton '62
Janet Slowik '84
George Sohn '86
Martin Solomon '61
Jan Solpera '85
Jeffrey Spear '83
Vic Spindler '73
Paul Standard** '86
Rolf Staudt '84
Walter Stanton '58
Murray Steiner '82
William Streever '50
Doug Stroup '83
Hansjorg Stulle '87
Ken Sweeny '78
William Taubin '56
Jack George Tauss '75
Pat Taylor '85
Anthony J. Teano '62
Bradbury Thompson '58
David Tregigda '85
Susan B. Trowbridge '82
Lucile Tuttle-Smith '78
Edward Vadala '72
Roger van den Bergh '86
Jan Van Der Ploeg '52
Dorothy Wachtenheim '86
Jurek Wajdowicz '80
Robert Wakeman '85
Herschel Wartik '59
Julian Waters '86
Professor Kurt Weidemann '66
Ken White '82
Cameron Williams '82
John F. Williamson '85
Conny Winter '85
Hal Zamboni* '47
Professor Hermann Zapf** '52
Roy Zucca '69

**Honorary Member
*Charter Member

Sustaining Members
Ad Agencies/Headliners '55
Allied Linotype '63
Arrow Typographers '75
Cardinal Type Service, Inc. '82
Characters Typographic Services, Inc. '85
Computer Telecommunications (CT)
  Typografix '86
International Typeface Corporation '80
Pastore DePamphilis Rampone '76
Photo-Lettering, Inc. '75
Royal Composing Room '55
Techni-Process Lettering '74
Typographic Designers '69
Typographic House '60
Typographic Images '86
TypoGraphic Innovations Inc. '72
TypoVision Plus '80

INDEX